EMERGENCY PREPAREDNESS

BOY SCOUTS OF AMERICA
IRVING, TEXAS

Note to the Counselor

The Boy Scouts of America believes that our youth need adult contacts to help them develop character, citizenship, and fitness. As a merit badge counselor, you have subscribed to these aims of Scouting.

The *Guide to Safe Scouting*, No. 34416, is updated every year and is available from your local council. Or, you can access it online at the official BSA Web site: *http://www.scouting.org*. As a merit badge counselor for Emergency Preparedness, this booklet may be particularly helpful to you. However, you should always review this document before any Scouting activities, including field trips and trips into the community.

Your BSA local council has both risk management and health and safety committees, or these two committees may be combined into one. Within the BSA, risk management is an administrative function (prevention and funding) and health and safety is a program function (assuring the implementation of safe programs). These committees may be able to help you as you plan Scouting activities in your community.

The protection of the young adults involved in Scouting is as important as the development of their career and hobby interests, which is the basic function of the merit badge program. Your active participation in and support of this goal is appreciated.

Requirements

1. Earn the First Aid merit badge.

2. Do the following:

   a. Discuss with your counselor these three aspects of emergency preparedness:

      (1) **Recognition** of a potential emergency situation

      (2) **Prevention** of an emergency situation

      (3) **Reaction** to an emergency situation

      Include in your discussion the kinds of questions that are important to ask yourself as you consider each of these.

   b. Make a chart that demonstrates your understanding of each of the three aspects of emergency preparedness in requirement 2a (recognition, prevention, and reaction) with regard to 10 of the situations listed below. **You must use situations 1, 2, 3, 4, and 5*** but may choose any other five for a total of 10 situations. Discuss this chart with your counselor.

      (1) Home kitchen fire*

      (2) Home basement/storage room/garage fire*

      (3) Explosion in the home*

      (4) Automobile accident*

      (5) Food-borne disease (food poisoning)*

      (6) Fire or explosion in a public place

      (7) Vehicle stalled in the desert

      (8) Vehicle trapped in a blizzard

      (9) Flash flooding in town or the country

      (10) Mountain/backcountry accident

     (11) Boating accident

     (12) Gas leak in a building

     (13) Tornado or hurricane

     (14) Major flood

     (15) Nuclear power plant emergency

     (16) Avalanche (snowslide or rockslide)

     (17) Violence in a public place

  c. Meet with and teach your family how to recognize, prevent, and react to the situations on the chart you created for requirement 2b. Then meet with your counselor and report on your family meeting, discussing their responses.

3. Show how you could safely save a person from the following:

  a. Touching a live electric wire

  b. A room filled with carbon monoxide

  c. Clothes on fire

  d. Drowning using nonswimming rescues (including accidents on ice)

4. Show three ways of attracting and communicating with rescue planes/aircraft.

5. With another person, show a good way to transport an injured person out of a remote and/or rugged area, conserving the energy of rescuers while ensuring the well-being and protection of the injured person.

6. Do the following:

  a. Tell the things a group of Scouts should be prepared to do, the training they need, and the safety precautions they should take for the following emergency services:

     (1) Crowd and traffic control

     (2) Messenger service and communication

     (3) Collection and distribution services

     (4) Group feeding, shelter, and sanitation

33368B
ISBN 0-8395-3368-3
©2003 Boy Scouts of America
2007 Printing

b. Identify the government or community agencies that normally handle and prepare for the emergency services listed under 6a, and explain to your counselor how a group of Scouts could volunteer to help in the event of these types of emergencies.

c. Find out who is your community's disaster/emergency response coordinator and learn what this person does to recognize, prevent, and respond to emergency situations in your community. Discuss this information with your counselor and apply what you discover to the chart you created for requirement 2b.

7. Take part in an emergency service project, either a real one or a practice drill, with a Scouting unit or a community agency.

8. Do the following:

a. Prepare a written plan for mobilizing your troop when needed to do emergency service. If there is already a plan, explain it. Tell your part in making it work.

b. Take part in at least one troop mobilization. Before the exercise, describe your part to your counselor. Afterward, conduct an "after-action" lesson, discussing what you learned during the exercise that required changes or adjustments to the plan.

c. Prepare a personal emergency service pack for a mobilization call. Prepare a family kit (suitcase or waterproof box) for use by your family in case an emergency evacuation is needed. Explain the needs and uses of the contents.

9. Do ONE of the following:

a. Using a safety checklist approved by your counselor, inspect your home for potential hazards. Explain the hazards you find and how they can be corrected.

b. Review or develop a plan of escape for your family in case of fire in your home.

c. Develop an accident prevention program for five family activities outside the home (such as taking a picnic or seeing a movie) that includes an analysis of possible hazards, a proposed plan to correct those hazards, and the reasons for the corrections you propose.

Contents

Introduction

In October 1989, baseball fans at the third game of the World Series between the Oakland A's and the San Francisco Giants had a big surprise: Just as the teams had finished batting practice, the bleachers suddenly shuddered with a rolling motion and rumbling echoed across the field. As a startled sportscaster said the feared word—"earthquake"—the TVs blacked out. Not realizing the seriousness of what was happening, fans cheered. One held up a sign reading: "That was nothing. Wait till the Giants bat!"

But nobody was cheering in nearby Oakland, where the top half of a double-decker highway collapsed. Buildings caved in, gas lines ruptured, fires broke out, and many people died or were injured that day.

After the northern California earthquake of 1989, Life Scout Ken McAfee of Troop 463 said, "I've seen pictures of the earthquake devastation many times on television, but you don't really know what it's like until you see it in person."

Throughout the Bay Area in the days and weeks that followed, members of the Boy Scouts of America responded. Cub Scouts collected food and clothing for The Salvation Army to distribute in the Marina district. Explorers staffed telephones at the Oakland police station, taking calls concerning missing persons. While rescue teams searched for survivors beneath the collapsed highway, Boy Scouts handed out food to workers and residents. Scouts and parents of Troop 463 in Sunnyvale distributed food and supplies for the more than 1,200 homeless people in Watsonville and worked at a disaster-relief center.

After the October quake, a local phone company published a full-page newspaper ad that encouraged area citizens to "learn from the Boy Scouts" and "Be Prepared."

Prepared for a Good Turn

After the terrorist attacks on the United States on September 11, 2001, thousands of American heroes emerged. Among the police officers, firefighters, and rescue workers who saved lives and worked around the clock during this pivotal moment in American history were other heroes who rallied for their country—Scouts.

The Boy Scouts of America commissioned artist Joseph Csatari to capture a lasting image of Scouts who were prepared for—and who responded to—this emergency. The painting, called "Prepared for a Good Turn," portrays Scouts working to provide relief alongside police officers and firefighters, and illustrates true stories of Scout heroes. Among them, Cub Scouts from Illinois who sent work gloves to the crew members at Ground Zero; Scouts from New York who donated cots for the relief workers to rest on at the site and collected bottled drinks to help refresh them; and Scouts in Oklahoma who started a "Helping Hands for Heroes" campaign to lend a hand to the families of those suddenly called into active military duty.

The Scout motto:

Be Prepared.

Nowhere do these words carry more meaning than in emergency preparedness. And these words, too, from the Scout Oath: *I will do my best . . . to help other people at all times.* And from the Scout Law: *A Scout is . . . helpful . . . brave.*

What is an *emergency*? Usually, it is something unforeseen, unexpected—something that requires immediate action. It can be related to weather, such a hurricane, a tornado, a snowstorm, or a flood; it can be an accident, such as an explosion, a fire, or a car accident. As a Scout, you should try never to be caught unprepared—especially for the unexpected—and you should try to learn the actions that can be helpful and needed before an emergency—what *preparedness* is all about—and during and after an emergency.

Scouts are often called upon to help because they know first aid and they know about the discipline and planning needed to support a situation that requires leadership. Scouting gives you the opportunity to understand and respond to your community's emergency preparedness plan. As you earn this merit badge, you will learn how to handle many emergency situations as an individual and as a member of a Scouting unit serving your neighborhood and community. Whether you may be needed as an active member of a community response team, or whether you provide enough skills and information to help protect your family, or yourself, from injury, everything you learn will help you be *brave* and *prepared* to *help other people at all times.*

Scouts Make a Difference

Scouts across the country help to make a difference during times of emergency. In Quincy, Massachusetts, Boy Scouts were part of a team of young people trained in first aid, CPR, traffic control, crowd management, communications, and lighting and power safety to help the citizens of Quincy during emergency and disaster situations.

In 1990, 60 miles from the epicenter of the 1989 earthquake in northern California, the community of Pacific Grove, California, decided to prepare a comprehensive earthquake and disaster plan after a study showed the likelihood of a complete loss of utilities, sewerage systems, and telephone services during an earthquake. A Volunteers in Preparedness program was formed to train neighborhood emergency response teams, which included Boy Scouts, in earthquake preparedness, disaster medicine, how and when to turn off natural gas service, how to rescue victims trapped under earthquake debris, and firefighting.

After Hurricane Georges devastated Puerto Rico in 1998, at the beginning of the 1999 hurricane season, 12 Puerto Rican Boy Scout troops went door-to-door to share with their neighbors some common-sense tips for preventing hurricane losses.

At the turn of the millennium, everyone faced the possibility of Y2K-related disasters. Minnesota Gov. Jesse Ventura borrowed the Scout motto in urging Minnesota families, businesses, and agencies to "Be Prepared" for possible century-end computer breakdowns. Scouts across the state went door-to-door to drop off Y2K preparedness cards that encouraged people to check whether home appliances would keep working, to keep financial records current, and to keep enough food and water on hand to last at least a week.

Recognition, Prevention, Reaction

In many ways, the world you live in today is much safer than the world in which your parents and grandparents grew up. Medical advances protect us from the emergencies caused by many diseases of the past; weather forecasting technology helps predict and protect us from dangerous weather conditions. We also learn about safety and preparedness from our experiences. For instance, the precautions taken for safe air travel in this country will forever be changed after the disasters of September 11, 2001.

Many institutions help us to be safer and deal with emergencies, too (see the resources section in this pamphlet). The Occupational Safety and Health Administration (OSHA) helps ensure safe and healthful workplaces for employees in the United States. The Federal Emergency Management Agency (FEMA) has the mission of helping citizens plan for and respond to disasters and emergencies of all kinds. The American Red Cross works around the world to help people in need. And the BSA publishes and regularly updates the *Guide to Safe Scouting,* which keeps your leaders informed about safe practices and emergency preparedness and response.

But it is not enough to rely on medicine, technology, institutions, or the actions of others to keep us prepared and safe. Part of being prepared for an emergency is looking carefully at your home and your community and educating yourself about potential dangers. As you read this merit badge pamphlet and work on your requirements, pay close attention to three things: recognition, prevention, and reaction.

Here are some examples of the kinds of questions you may ask yourself as you look around you:

1. Ask yourself questions that will help you **recognize** a risky situation or possibility of an emergency or accident occurring.

   - Do I live in an area that may experience dangerous weather (hurricanes, tornadoes, blizzard conditions)? During what time of year? Is my area prone to earthquakes or flooding?

   - Is my family car in good working order? Are any of the electrical outlets in my home overloaded with too many plugs? Are materials that burn easily (those that are *flammable*), such as charcoal lighter fluid, stored safely?

   - Is food properly refrigerated, stored, and prepared in my home?

What is *preparedness?* The Federal Emergency Management Agency, or FEMA, says that "preparedness provides leadership, training, readiness, and exercise support, and technical and financial assistance to strengthen citizens; communities; state, local, and tribal governments; and professional emergency workers as they prepare for disasters, mitigate [relieve or lessen] the effects of disasters, respond to community needs after a disaster, and launch effective recovery efforts." You can visit the FEMA Web site and learn a lot more about preparedness at *http://www.fema.gov.*

2. Ask yourself questions that will help you **prevent** a dangerous situation or emergency when you can.

   • What can I do to make my home safer from fire or explosion?

   • How can I help minimize, or lessen, the damage that might be caused during an emergency (during violent weather, for instance)? Can I help make sure that no one would be injured?

   • Can I help make sure that people are acting in a safe manner during a situation, say, when I'm hiking with my troop in the wilderness?

3. Ask yourself questions that will help you **react to** an emergency situation in the best way you can.

   • How can I react *before* a crisis? How can I prepare for it if it were to happen? Can I gather and position supplies that might be needed? Can I help educate and train people about safety and preparedness?

   • How can I react *after* a crisis? Is there a family or community plan for reaction that I should know about? What resources might be mobilized and needed, and how can I help?

Three Aspects of Emergency Preparedness

This is what emergency preparedness is all about: recognizing, preventing, and reacting to the unexpected. Emergencies can be met and handled. Whether an emergency involves your family or your entire community, on highways or waterways, in your home or outdoors, you can bring your Scouting skills and knowledge to the situation and help. Recreate this chart to help you complete requirement 2.

Emergency Situation	Recognition	Prevention	Reaction
Fire in the home			
Tornado			
Car accident			

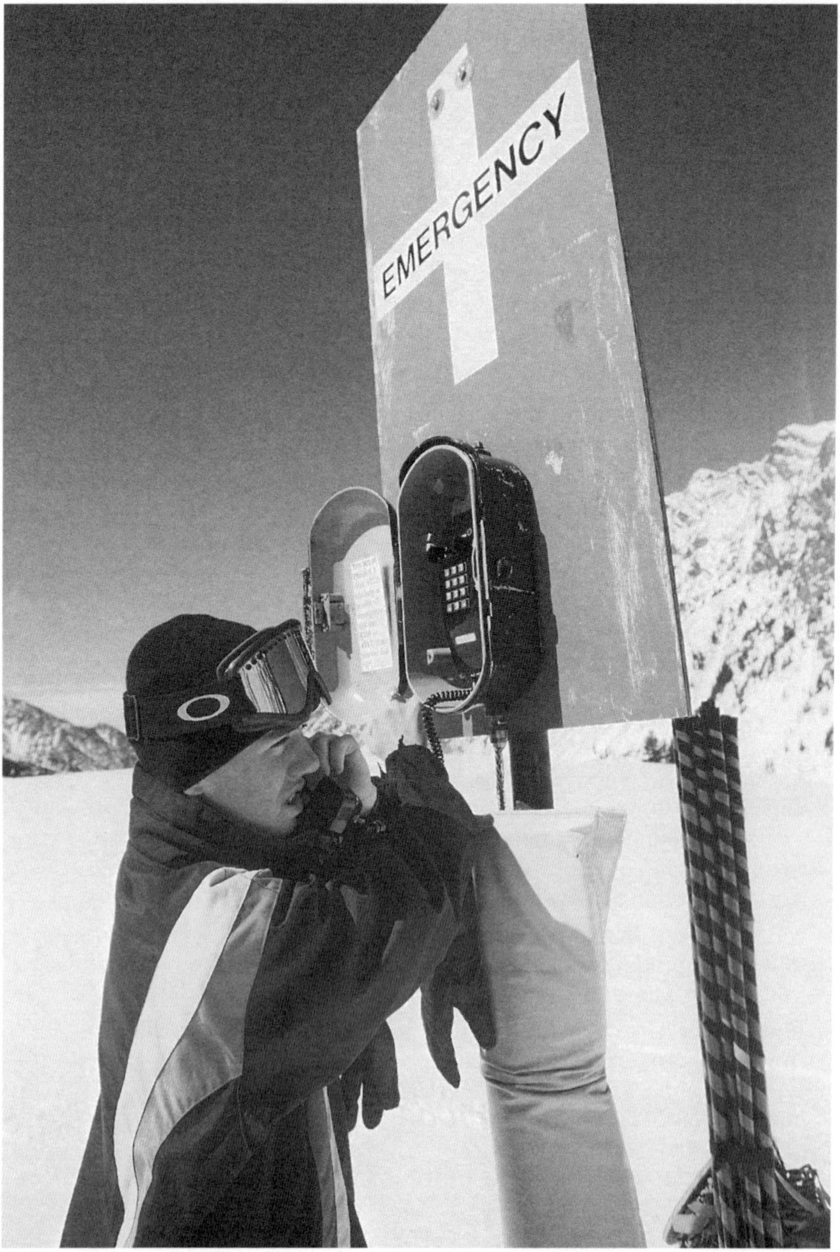
EMERGENCY

First Aid First

The first requirement for this merit badge is to earn the First Aid merit badge, because first aid is emergency preparedness in action. You need to *recognize* what is wrong with a person and then *react to* the emergency with the correct treatment until medical help arrives.

You should know first aid so well that you would be able to react to any situation immediately. What would you do in these situations?

- You're eating pizza with some friends. Suddenly, your friend's little sister darts in and grabs some pizza. As she runs away giggling and eating, she trips and starts choking. She turns blue and stops breathing.

- You're camping out with your patrol. During some free time, you offer to take a new patrol member on a hike around the lake. When you're halfway around the lake, he says his heel is so sore he can hardly walk. He takes off his shoe (he's wearing old running shoes rather than sturdy hiking boots) and finds a huge blister. You have 2 miles to walk in either direction to get back to camp and the first-aid kit.

- You're horsing around with friends indoors on a rainy day. One buddy pushes another and he falls into a glass-topped coffee table. The glass shatters and gashes his wrist. Blood starts spurting out.

- You're skateboarding on the riverwalk with a friend. His board hits a crack and he's thrown from it. He's not wearing a helmet; his head hits the cement bank, and he falls into the water. He's floating facedown.

Now look at the situations again, and ask yourself how you might have helped to *prevent* them—another important part of emergency preparedness.

These emergencies call for *immediate action*. If you have already earned the First Aid merit badge, review those skills so that you will be prepared to use them in an emergency.

The Boy Scouts of America recommends the following first-aid procedures to guard against blood-borne viruses:

Treat all blood as if it is contaminated with blood-borne viruses. Do not use bare hands to stop bleeding; always use a protective barrier and always wash exposed skin areas with hot water and soap immediately after treating a victim. Include the following pieces of equipment in all first-aid kits, and use them when giving first aid:

- Latex, vinyl, or nitrile gloves, to be used when stopping bleeding or dressing wounds

- A mouth-barrier device, for giving rescue breathing or cardiopulmonary resuscitation (CPR)

- Plastic goggles or other eye protection, to prevent a victim's blood from getting into a rescuer's eyes in the event of serious arterial bleeding

- Antiseptic, for sterilizing or cleaning exposed skin areas, particularly if soap and water are not available

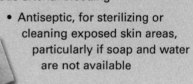

Emergency in the Home

Fire or Explosion

"An ounce of prevention is worth a pound of cure"—so goes the old saying. And *recognizing* potentially hazardous situations that might lead to fire or explosion is the first step on the road to prevention.

Fire Safety in the Home

How safe from fire or explosion is your home? You can do a lot to prevent these situations. With help from your family, get rid of hazards. Clear closets, the attic, the cellar, and storage areas of flammable rubbish such as papers and empty cartons. Check around the furnace, and move anything that could burn—such as paint or paper—at least 3 feet away from it.

Throw out half-empty cans of paint and varnish, paint-soaked brushes, and oily rags. Keep turpentine and paint thinners in airtight cans. Gasoline, benzene, naphtha, charcoal lighter fluid, camp-stove fuel, and other highly flammable liquids should be kept in tightly closed metal containers outside of the home. Throw out any trash that has collected around the yard.

Check with local authorities such as the city's sanitation department about how to dispose of flammable materials. In some areas, you may need to take them to a special drop-off location because they may not be thrown out with regular household trash.

You can do much to protect your home from fire by finding potential hazards (recognition) and getting rid of them or otherwise making them safe (prevention and reaction before a disaster).

Be alert to electrical fire hazards. If you find frayed cords, bare wires, or broken plugs in your home, suggest to your parents that these should be replaced. Do you have too many appliances, electronic gadgets, lamps, radios, or televisions plugged into one circuit? Get rid of "octopuses" (multiple-circuit adapters). This would be a good time to have a family talk about the electrical system and use of electricity in your home.

Fires can start even when safety measures are taken. Fire emergencies are more common than any other kind of emergency, so every family should have a fire escape plan. Develop one for your family that details two ways out of each room in your home. Make sure your family has an escape ladder at each window in bedrooms above the first floor. Test your smoke alarms once a month, and replace the batteries once a year. Talk about what you would do if your home caught on fire.

For further reference and more fire preparedness ideas, see the "Fire Safety Checklist" in the *Fire Safety* merit badge pamphlet.

Practice Before It Happens

Practice fire escape drills at least once a year. Pick a place outside where your family can meet if a fire breaks out. (You will find more information about a family escape plan in the *Safety* merit badge pamphlet.)

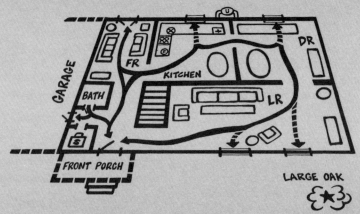

Draw a floor plan of your home to help you plot emergency escape routes and a meeting place outdoors for all family members.

In an Emergency, Use the Phone

In many emergency situations, the first and smartest thing you can do is *call for help*. In your home, post emergency numbers (such as the fire department, police, and doctor) by all phones. Calling the 9-1-1 emergency number will summon fire, police, and ambulance services. Tell the 9-1-1 operator your name and address and what the emergency is; then stay on the line until you are sure help is on the way.

If 9-1-1 service is not available in your area, dial "0" and tell the operator your address and your emergency.

Life-Saving Fire Safety Tips

If you know how to react in the event of a fire in your home, you can prevent injuries and possibly save lives. Teach these tips to your family and discuss them:

1. If there is a fire, warn everyone possible—without endangering your own safety.

2. Keep calm. Walk fast. Do not run.

3. If 9-1-1 service is not available in your area and you can't find the number for the fire department, dial "0" and tell the operator, "I want to report a fire." *Tell the operator your address.*

4. If you can't get to a phone, call for help from a window. Wave a towel to signal for attention.

5. Keep doors closed. Open doors and windows cause drafts that can fan a fire and make it more serious. If you think the door is the only way out, feel it. If it is hot, do not open it. If it is not hot, duck to one side when you turn the knob. Open the door slowly. If the door opens inward, brace it with your foot to keep it from opening too fast.

6. If there is smoke in a room, crawl close to the floor. The air is least toxic about 12 to 18 inches above the floor. If you can't see well, keep the back of one hand in front of you. Using your hand, follow the wall around to the nearest door or window.

7. If you can walk downstairs, do it carefully—preferably backward and close to the wall.

8. Buildings that are two or three stories high should have an escape ladder. If you do not have one, and you or others are trapped on the second or third floor, tie sheets and blankets together using the sheet bend knot. Tie one end to a heavy piece of furniture, drop the other end out of a window, and climb down. Otherwise, get a sheet or other bright cloth and hang it outside a window to get the attention of people outside. Stay by the window and wait for the fire department to arrive and rescue you. Avoid the urge to jump out of the window—wait for help to arrive. Push towels or clothes against the bottom of the door to keep smoke from entering the room.

9. *Absolutely never use an elevator during a fire.*

10. Remember that children may become very scared and hide under beds or in closets. You can make sure that they practice a fire escape plan so they know the right thing to do in case of a fire.

11. Do not delay your escape by trying to rescue someone else. *In an emergency, you are never a hero by placing yourself in danger!* Get out of the burning building to save yourself. Meet the fire department when it arrives, and tell firefighters where you last saw other people.

During a fire, feel doors and don't open them if they are hot. Keep your nose and mouth covered with a clean cloth to help prevent you from breathing in smoke and other toxic fumes.

Because firefighters have training, protective clothing, and breathing apparatus, they will be better able to rescue someone—and you will be most helpful by letting them know where other people need their expert assistance.

Most of the points above are just as important to know for a fire emergency anywhere, such as in a public building. Look them over again and think about how they might apply. And here are two more important points:

- Never go inside a building that is on fire. Wait for the fire department to arrive with the right equipment and gear to rescue people and put the fire out.

- You probably have regular fire drills at school. This is emergency preparedness in action. If you are in school when a fire breaks out, follow your teacher's instructions. Do not go out on your own.

Gas Leak

Gas fumes can kill. Garages, basements, and kitchens are the danger spots in a home. Fumes from leaky gas pipes, ovens, stoves, and bad connections for furnaces, clothes dryers, water heaters, and other gas appliances can cause a person to stop breathing, followed by unconsciousness and death.

Stoves that are left on but not lighted are especially hazardous. If anyone creates a spark in a fume-filled room, an explosion will follow. Gas fumes also can come from other sources, such as an improperly "banked" coal furnace or the exhaust from a car or truck.

Smart homeowners have gas fixtures and appliances inspected regularly and keep them in good repair. Have your parents check the gas pipes in your home, especially in damp areas such as the basement, to make sure that they are not rusting. Use a flashlight when making your checks—incredibly, some people risk deadly explosion by searching for leaks with a match! Natural gas also has a distinctive odor that you can smell.

If someone becomes overcome by gas fumes, get the person outdoors into fresh air. If the person has stopped breathing, immediately give rescue breathing (see the *First Aid* merit badge pamphlet). Call 9-1-1 or the fire department or rescue squad. Notify the gas company.

If you smell gas or suspect a leak and your parents are not home, open windows and get everyone outdoors. Call the gas company immediately.

Emergency in Your Car

If you get trapped somewhere while traveling, remember that your car horn can alert rescuers as far as a mile downwind.

Road trips with your family or with your troop can be great fun. But they need to be safe, too, especially because you might be far from home or from immediate help as you travel. So preparation is very important.

- Consider the weather you might encounter. Prepare for the worst. Check weather reports and plan travel routes accordingly. If severe weather is threatening, consider delaying your trip.

- Keep at least half a tank of gasoline in the car.

- Before you leave, let others know your route and when you expect to arrive.

- Pack food, water, medications, and extra clothing (appropriate for the season and weather conditions).

- Keep a first-aid kit, flares, and booster cables in your car.

- Always buckle up—every time, every seat, every person.

You can check out the *Traffic Safety* merit badge pamphlet for more information about recognizing and preventing emergency situations in vehicles.

Motor Vehicle Accident

Sometimes, accidents just happen. As always, be prepared for the unexpected. With a motor vehicle accident, often the most important thing you can do is get yourself into a first-aid mind-set. Is anyone hurt? Is anyone bleeding badly? Is anyone dazed or in shock? In your work for the First Aid merit badge, you learned how to respond to such situations.

The leading killer of Scout-age boys is motor vehicle accidents. The more you can do to recognize potentially hazardous conditions that might contribute to an accident, the more you can help save lives.

Some people may want to move accident victims or rush them to a hospital. Urge them not to do so; victims should stay lying down (if possible) until medical help arrives. If help does not come quickly, check for fractures. If you know how, splint to keep the fractured part from moving and help reduce pain and prevent shock.

Four things are essential to help prevent further injury and loss of life:

1. Call for medical help.

2. Make the scene safe: Turn off the vehicle's engine, secure parking brakes, help direct traffic. **Note:** If you can't readily secure the scene, *do not put yourself in danger trying to do so.*

3. Stop severe bleeding.

4. Treat for shock.

Trapped in a Blizzard

If you find yourself trapped in a blizzard, use your ingenuity and always ask yourself, *What is the* safest *thing to do*? Stay with the car and wait for help. Leave your car *only* if you are sure of the way to the nearest building and you know that it is a short distance away. But wait for the blizzard conditions to lessen, too. Do not walk in a blizzard. It is easy to lose sight of your car and become lost in blowing snow.

If you are on a well-traveled road, show a "trouble" signal. To attract rescuers, set hazard lights to the flashing mode or hang a bright cloth from the radio antenna or window.

When traveling in severe cold weather, keep the following in your car:

- Blankets (or sleeping bags)

- Snow shovel (at least one)

- Tire chains

- Siphon hose

- Ice scraper

- Bottled water

- High-energy snack foods, such as candy bars

If possible, run the engine and heater just long enough to remove the chill from the air—about 10 minutes each hour. Conserve gasoline. But be careful when running the engine, too: Do not let the exhaust pipe get clogged with snow. Blockage can cause deadly carbon monoxide to leak into the passenger compartment. For ventilation, open your window slightly on the side away from the wind. Occasionally, breathe deeply and rapidly move your arms and legs to increase blood circulation.

The inside of a car can protect you for a time. At night, keep the inside dome light on. It uses only a small amount of current from the battery, and it will make it easier for rescuers to see the car in the dark.

If you are stuck for more than six hours and the cold in the car becomes too much to bear, consider moving into a snow hole or snow shelter. The temperature inside a snow hole can be 15 to 20 degrees warmer than the air outside the hole. For more information about cold-weather shelters, see the *Wilderness Survival* merit badge pamphlet.

Scouts are known for their resourcefulness. Look around and make do with what you have. You could use the flat, round top of the air cleaner in your car for digging in the snow. Use a cushion from the car as a seat in your snow hole, or cut branches from a tree. (You will need a seat so that you are not sitting in melted snow; stay as dry as possible.) As soon as you can, build a fire outside (not in the shelter). Use the car's spare tire or hubcaps as a fireplace, or place logs on top of the snow. You might be able to start a fire with the car's lighter. For tinder, tear up road maps or other paper you might have in the car, or strip fabric from the car seats. If you do not have fuel for a fire, look through the car again. Wooden handles of tools will burn, for instance.

You may have heard that the universal distress signal "SOS" stands for "Save Our Ship" or "Save Our Souls," but it turns out that this is just a myth. The Berlin Radiotelegraphic Conference of 1906 adopted SOS as a danger signal merely because the Morse code for SOS—three dots, three dashes, and three dots—was felt to be unmistakable when relayed by telegraph. These days, "three" can mean "distress" in other contexts, too, such as lighting three fires to indicate distress or arranging three piles of debris that searchers might see.

Make three small fires arranged in a triangle as a distress signal. If you can't build a fire, stamp out a big "SOS" in the snow near your car. Make the letters deep so that shadows are cast into them, making them easier for rescuers to see.

If you are stuck with your car for more than a day, finding food and water could become a problem. You can get water by melting or eating clean snow. If you do not have any food, work slowly and rest often. If you do not rest while in extremely cold weather, you will tire quickly and become exhausted.

Know your route when you travel and plan for weather conditions or terrain—such as snow and cold or desert and heat—that might unexpectedly become dangerous.

Stalled in the Desert

If your car stalls in the desert, stay *with* the car but not *in* it. If you are on a regularly traveled road, someone will come by soon to help. At night, attract attention any way you can: Set out an emergency light, turn on the car flashers or turn signals, leave the inside dome light on or, if possible, build a fire.

If you are stalled in a remote desert area, stay with the car. Sit in its shade. Stay calm and think; do not act hastily. You will need water and you will need to protect yourself from the heat. Stay covered; do not throw away clothing, no matter how hot it gets. Clothing will guard against the sun, blowing sand, and insects.

Water is the most important thing. Know these potential sources of water:

- **Dew.** If the night is cold, in the morning you can collect the dew that forms on cars, rocks, and plants.

- **Cactus.** Cut off cactus sections and mash them in a container. Eat the cactus pulp. Slice off the top of big barrel cactuses and scoop out the water inside.

- **Desert plants.** Dig up the roots of desert plants, peel them, and eat the pulp.

- **Water holes.** In the evening and early morning, listen for birds and watch for circling flocks and freshly made animal tracks. Follow the birds or tracks—they can lead to water. *Caution:* Salty or soapy-tasting water may be poisonous. (But you may be able to treat it with a solar still; see the plan later in this chapter.)

If you must walk in search of things, leave a note at the car telling anyone who arrives the direction you went. Walk only after sundown. Rest during the day in any shade that you can find or make.

In truly desperate situations, burying yourself in sand can keep you cooler. The temperature 1 foot below the ground surface can be as much as 18 degrees cooler than above ground.

Use signal fires to attract the attention of planes or other desert travelers. Use the car mirror as a signaling device as described in the "Plane Signals" section later in this pamphlet. Spell out "SOS" on the ground with rags or strips of car seat covering—or anything that you can find that is dark.

> If you find water, drink it. Do not ration it. Trying to make it last longer does more harm than good. Do not eat food unless you drink at least a pint of water a day.

Solar Still

With plastic sheeting, you can make a solar still. You can get up to 3 pints of water a day using a 6-foot-square sheet of plastic.

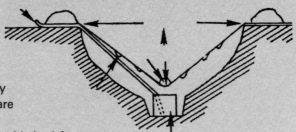

Dig a pit 4 feet wide by 3 feet deep. Place a shallow container in the center of the pit. If possible, rig a tube from the container up to the edge of the pit. Stretch clear plastic over the pit, and then place a rock in the center to form a cone directly over the container. Secure the edges of the plastic tightly with rocks or soil all the way around. Solar heat evaporates moisture from the ground, which condenses on the plastic and drips into the container. (Split cactus stems laid around the inside will increase the moisture and improve the water yield.) Draw water through the tube to avoid disturbing the still.

This still can also treat brackish (salty) or tainted water. In fact, you can distill water from just about anything—even urine.

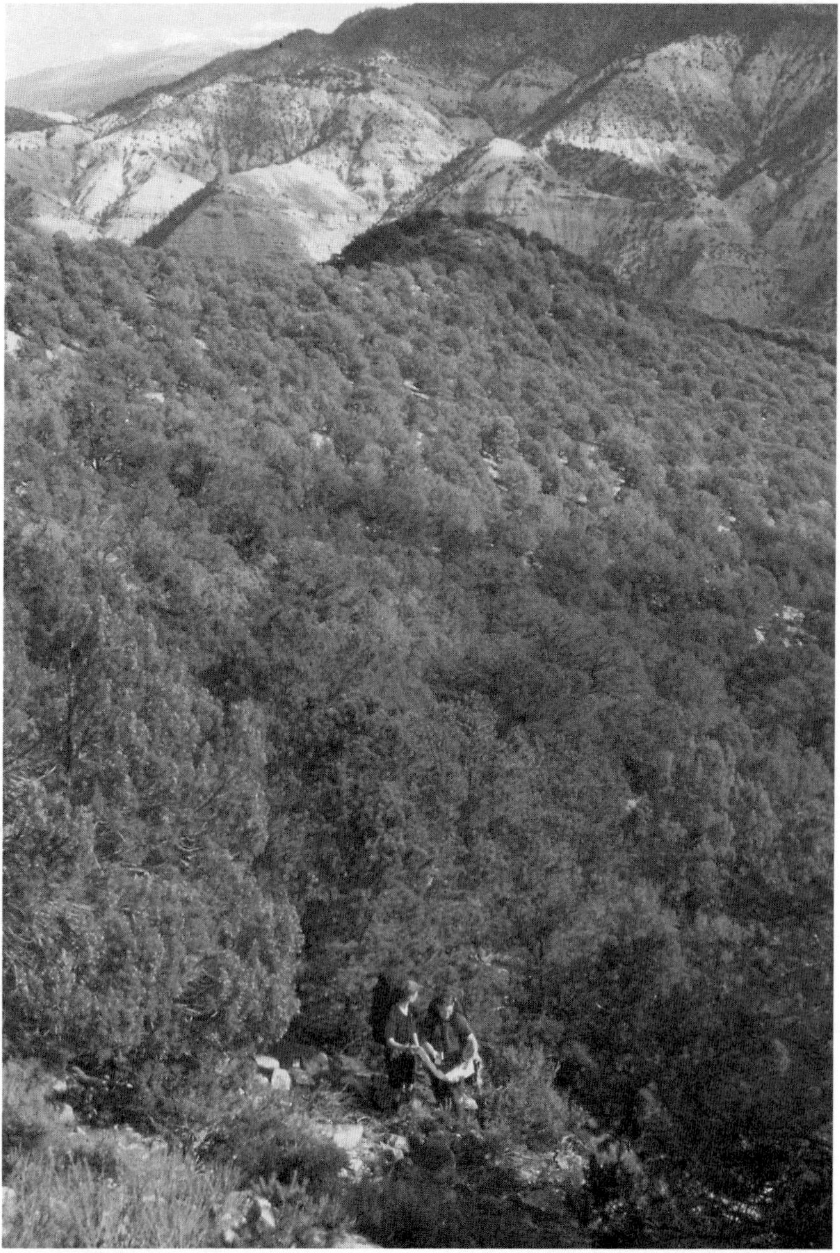

Emergency in the Outdoors

Mountain/Backcountry Accident

Try to anticipate and recognize what hazards you might face before you leave on a wilderness trip by studying a map of the area where you are going. Know the terrain. Take the map with you, and always tell someone where you are going and when.

The best way to help prevent injury or loss of life on a mountain or backcountry trip (or any hiking, for that matter) is to follow the "rule of three": Do not travel alone; one buddy is good, but three or more hiking together is better. If one person gets hurt, the second can perform first aid and stay with the victim while the third can get help. Following this guideline also will reduce your chances of getting lost.

Carry a first-aid kit as well as a survival kit that has items such as hooks and lines, emergency food, and a plastic bag for water storage. Remember to bring basic hiking necessities, such as a pocketknife, compass, waterproofed matches, and adhesive bandages.

You can help prevent mountain accidents by having the right equipment and clothing—along with emergency supplies—before you set out.

Watch Where You Step

Do not travel after dark, and stay on trails. A hiker in Washington left a marked trail on Mount Si to follow a mountain goat. But mountain goats are better at off-trail hiking than people are. This hiker jumped to a ledge he could not escape and had to spend the night there—along with a lot of hungry mosquitoes.

Stay on Your Feet

In the mountains or backcountry, the most common accident is a fall. Try to prevent them. When going down a hill or a steep bank, control your center of gravity; that is, lean back slightly. If you fall, you will fall backward, and then you will be in a sliding, rather than a tumbling, position. Leaning forward and grabbing branches or other objects for support is not always a good idea. The support might give way, roll, break, or slide—and then you will tumble forward.

In rough-going areas, try to anticipate where you might fall. That way, if you do fall, you will at least fall in the safest place and manner.

Stay off fallen timber, which can be wet and mossy, making for a slippery surface. Likewise, wet rocks can be slick and dangerous. Even if you don't fall over, you can twist an ankle.

Weather

Watch for lightning and thunderstorms. Take shelter in a low area under a thick growth of small trees. Don't stand under a tall, isolated tree in an open space.

If you must wade across a stream, study it carefully first, finding the safest place to cross. Carry a staff (hiker's pole), which you can use for support if the current is swift. Test the bottom of the stream with the pole as you cross. Loosen pack straps before you cross so that you can get the pack off easily if trouble develops.

You are safer in a mountain forest than you are on a treeless slope. If you are in an alpine meadow, head for the lowest spot of the nearest forest cover. If you get caught in a storm where you can't quickly get to a low, safe spot, be a small target: Crouch and place your hands on your knees with your head between them until the storm passes. Don't lie flat on the ground, which will make you a larger target.

Don't camp in a gully or dry streambed. A thunderstorm or flash flood miles away could send a rushing torrent of water through your campsite.

Lost or Marooned

If you become lost or marooned with a group, such as your patrol, be a leader. Stay calm and help others stay calm. Tell everyone to sit and think. Clear an area on the ground and "build" a map to help you estimate where you are. Mark landmarks that you can see. Try to reconstruct your trail on the map. How long have you been gone? Can anyone remember when and where he last saw something familiar—a scarred tree? a creek or pond? a fence? Put it on your map. Discuss every detail about your hike that anyone can remember.

Rest and consider your options. Usually, it is best to stay put. In a way, *you* are not lost—the people searching for you are, and their chances of finding you are greater than your chances of finding them.

If you must travel and everyone agrees to it, walk in a straight line. Use the sighting system: If you can get to a high point safely, go up and look over the land below, find a familiar landmark, and head toward it. Leave a note or otherwise indicate your direction of travel for searchers.

If there is any possibility that you will have to stay out overnight, find a good campsite before dusk. Do not travel at night.

You can help prevent getting lost by always using the buddy system when you hike and knowing how to read a compass and use a map.

Plane Signals

Three of anything —visual or audible—repeated at regular intervals is a distress signal. The distress *answer* is two of anything.

If you are lost, you might need to get the attention of a rescue plane. Fire and smoke get a pilot's attention. Three fires arranged in a triangle convey a universal SOS. Build fires in an open area where they can be seen. Keep a pile of fuel (brush, twigs, leaves, grass) nearby so that you can quickly make the fires bigger. If you are short of fuel, lay a fire and be ready to light it when you first hear a plane.

Smoky fires show wind direction. This could be helpful to a pilot who has a chance to land. You can make a fire smoke by throwing on it green wood, wet or damp leaves, decayed wood, rubber, or fuel oil.

With a smoky fire you can send smoke signals. Cut off the smoke with a wet blanket (or something similar). Release it, but quickly cut off the smoke again. Do this so that you send three short puffs in a row. Pause and repeat.

"Three" means "distress." A pilot might spot three piles of debris when looking for a lost person. Three piles of cut branches or rocks might work. Flashing SOS using Morse code—three short flashes, three long flashes (twice as long as the short ones), three short flashes—is another way to attract help, night or day.

One way to get the attention of a rescue plane is to use a mirror to aim a beam of reflected sunlight at the plane (see the sidebar on signaling with a mirror). If you don't see a plane, sweep the horizon with your reflected sunbeam anyway. This tiny flash of light can be seen for 50 or more miles.

You can make a signaling mirror with a knife and an empty can. Cut out the lid or bottom of the can, punch a hole in the center, and you are ready to signal. You can also use the blade of your knife. If you are lost and have none of this equipment, you could use a smooth, wet piece of wood, a flat rock, or anything that will reflect some sunlight.

Signaling with a mirror can save your life, but you must know how to aim it effectively toward your rescuer. Hold the mirror close to your face and toward your signal target. Hold your other hand outstretched in front of you as a sight line and make a V with your fingers. Move the mirror so that the sun reflects from the mirror onto your outstretched hand and through the V, and then move your hand and the mirror together and point them toward your target.

Take time to practice signaling with a mirror. Try it with a buddy in the distance as your "rescuer" and signal to one another.

A ground-level "sign language" of symbols can attract an aircraft and communicate with the pilot (see the illustrations). Make the symbols with strips of cloth, rocks, or branches—any available material that will contrast with the background that it is placed on. Make the symbols big—10 feet wide or wider—in an open area where they can be seen. You can also stamp the symbols in sand or snow. If possible, line the bottom of such tracks with something dark, such as leafy green branches. Pile sand or snow on one side so that the sun will throw a shadow onto the symbols.

When in doubt, use the international distress symbol, SOS.

An X is the ground-air visual code meaning "Require medical assistance."

You can also "talk" to a pilot with body signals. Most pilots know this universal language. Learn the 11 standard body signals illustrated in this chapter.

Know how to "read" a pilot, too. A pilot says "yes" by dipping the nose of the plane up and down. Zigzagging—or fishtailing—the plane means "no." If your message has been understood, the pilot will rock the plane from side to side or flash green lights with a signal lamp. If your message has not been understood, the pilot will make a complete right-hand circle or flash red lights.

Ground-Air Visual Code for Use by Survivors

V	X	N	Y	↑
REQUIRE ASSISTANCE	REQUIRE MEDICAL ASSISTANCE	NO	YES	PROCEEDING IN THIS DIRECTION

Ground-Air Visual Code for Use by Search Parties

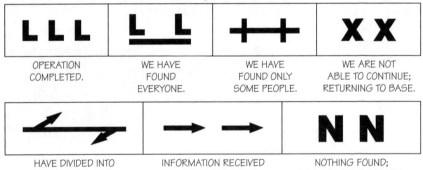

L L L	L⌐ ⌐L	┼─┼	X X
OPERATION COMPLETED.	WE HAVE FOUND EVERYONE.	WE HAVE FOUND ONLY SOME PEOPLE.	WE ARE NOT ABLE TO CONTINUE; RETURNING TO BASE.

⟵⟶	→ →	N N
HAVE DIVIDED INTO TWO GROUPS, EACH PROCEEDING IN DIRECTION INDICATED.	INFORMATION RECEIVED THAT AIRCRAFT IS IN THIS DIRECTION.	NOTHING FOUND; WILL CONTINUE SEARCH.

Standard Body Signals

PICK US UP, AIR-CRAFT ABANDONED.

DO NOT TRY TO LAND HERE.

ALL OK; DO NOT WAIT.

AFFIRMATIVE (YES).

USE DROP MESSAGE.

OUR RECEIVER IS OPERATING.

NEED MECHANICAL HELP OR PARTS—LONG DELAY.

NEGATIVE (NO).

CAN PROCEED SHORTLY; WAIT IF PRACTICAL.

URGENTLY NEED MEDICAL ASSISTANCE.

LAND HERE (POINT IN DIRECTION OF LANDING).

Search and Rescue

In places where people get lost frequently, such as in mountainous or wilderness areas, volunteer search-and-rescue teams have formed to meet the need. Searchers in helicopters and on horseback, as well as trained dogs, all try to find lost people. In some places, Scouts and Venturers have specialized search-and-rescue activities and participate actively in operations. If your troop is called to be part of a search-and-rescue team, you must be familiar with basic search tactics and detection methods.

Search Tactics

A search director, such as a deputy sheriff or other official, will handle the overall planning for a search. A basic search plan will follow something similar to this five-step sequence:

1. **Preliminary.** Searchers receive their assignments and information about the lost person (or people): Where was the person last seen? Did he or she have wilderness experience? How was the person dressed, and what equipment did he or she have?

2. **Confinement.** It is important to try to keep the lost person from wandering outside of a known area. Barricades and string lines might be used. Searchers may be assigned to block roads or trails.

3. **Detection.** Searchers need to discover anything within the confined area that might help find the lost person. See the "Lost-Person Search Method" sidebar for one kind of structured grid sweep of an area.

4. **Tracking.** Dogs sometimes are used to track a lost person. Skilled searchers can follow footprints and know how to read other tracking signs.

5. **Evacuation.** When found, the lost person needs to be treated for injuries, if any, and evacuated.

Lost-Person Search Method

Type A sweep
Three teams shown

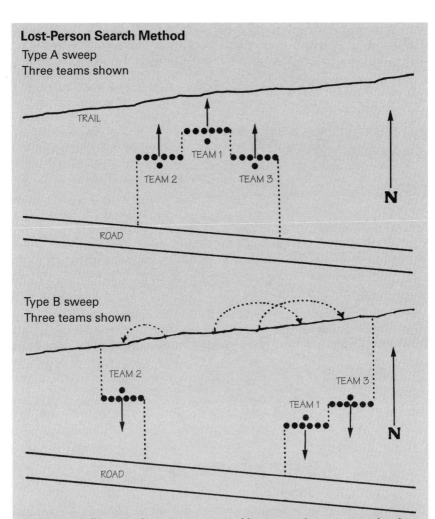

In these two diagrams, three teams are searching an area between a road and a trail. Team 1 lays ribbon lines (dotted lines) at the edges of its search lanes. Teams 2 and 3 pick up the ribbons and move them to the edges of their search lanes as they begin searching. The area behind the teams is therefore clearly identified as having been searched, and the area outside the ribbons is identified for the "pivot" and continuing search pattern.

When teams pivot to continue the search, they move to the sides (shown by the dotted arrows) to the outside of the ribbons. Teams move the ribbons again to the outside of the search pattern. As they continue "sweeping" in this way, the searched area will expand farther to the left and right.

Along with the detection method shown in the sidebar, a simple search might involve a large number of small teams checking natural and artificial features in an area. This could include trail checks (hiking a trail to see whether the lost person is walking it), ridge-running (taking a quick route along high ground to search valleys from above), and checking buildings, drainage areas, caves, or other potential hazards. The emphasis is on making a quick check of the most obvious places a person may get lost.

Avalanche

An avalanche is a mass of snow, earth, rock, or other material that sweeps down a mountainside or precipice. They are sometimes called snowslides, rockslides, or landslides.

The best way to protect yourself against any kind of avalanche is to avoid climbing or skiing in dangerous high country without an experienced guide. Experienced climbers and hikers know how to identify and avoid places where snowslides or rockslides might start.

The force of an avalanche of snow can snap tree trunks as if they were matchsticks.

Rockslides

- Do not ever throw rocks in high country, or worse yet, push boulders off a high cliff. Falling rocks will hit and loosen other rocks, and before you know it, a rockslide could be tumbling down.

- Loose rocks are most likely to fall when early morning sun melts any ice that held the rocks in place on rocky slopes.

- Heavy rains can weaken the soil that cements rocks together. During rainstorms, do not hike, stand, or camp in the fall zone of a cliff.

- Know the different types of rock. For example, sandstone and shale break apart easily.

- You will often find piles of rocks, called *talus*, at the base of cliffs. Avoid talus slopes when you can. If you must cross one, do so carefully. Do not walk directly behind someone else.

- As with all backcountry hiking, stick to trails. Do not take shortcuts or cut across switchbacks.

Snowslides

According to FEMA, about 19 people die every year in snowslides in the United States. As skiing and snowmobiling become more popular in more areas, snowslides will become more common—unless people always take precautions that can help prevent them.

- Stay out of the mountains after a heavy snowfall or strong, windy storm. Let the snow settle for at least three days. Check state and local avalanche advisories before going out. The U.S. Forest Service can help.

- Stay off slopes that face the sun, which will melt the snow and make it more dangerous.

- If there is high avalanche risk, avoid the backcountry. Within ski area boundaries, the snowpack is carefully managed.

- Avoid the bottoms of narrow valleys, ravines, and gulches, especially if they are below steep slopes.

- Always use the buddy system, and carry a shovel, snow probe, and transceiver for communication. You can learn to judge the "character" of snow with the probe.

If you find yourself on a snow slab or other avalanche danger spot, go straight downward or upward—not across. Move one person at a time. If you are likely to fall on your skis, it would be safer to remove them and not fall.

Experienced alpine skiers tie a 30-yard red cord to their belts and trail this behind them as they ski. If they are caught in a snowslide, the cord will float to the surface of the snow where rescuers can spot it.

If you are caught in a snowslide, try to get your skis off and "swim" on the surface on your back with your feet pointed downhill. Just before the snow comes to a standstill, use every bit of strength you have to force your head to the surface.

If you see others caught in a snowslide, watch carefully so you will be able to tell rescuers the general area where they disappeared. Also, keep an eye out for a second slide, which often follows the first.

Boating Accident

The two main causes of boating injuries are

- Not having Coast Guard–approved personal flotation devices (PFDs, or life jackets) for *everyone* on board a boat—and not *wearing* the PFDs

  - Not keeping a proper lookout; that is, not paying attention to where the boat is going and then ramming into something

If your family has a boat, check the equipment and make sure it and the boat are in good repair and working order. If you have a powerboat, carry fire extinguishers, proper lights, an extra paddle, and an anchor. Chain outboard motors to the boat. Know the boat's *capacity*—the number of people it can carry safely—which is shown on a metal plate on the boat. Do not take more people aboard than the stated capacity.

If you must move around in a boat, stay low and in the center and hold on to the sides. If your boat capsizes, hang on to it unless it is on fire. Wait for help. Do not try to swim for land. It is easier for rescuers to see a capsized boat than a lone swimmer.

Observe the rules for water travel (see the *Motorboating* merit badge pamphlet). Do not run a motorboat through or close to a swimming area. When you approach a landing place, slow to a speed less than 5 miles per hour.

Keep an eye on the weather. Head for home—or the nearest place where you can tie up—*before* a storm reaches you.

Know standard distress codes, calls, and signals so that if you have an accident, you can give the proper call. If you have a radiotelephone, you can send official distress calls, such as the standard "Mayday." Repeat the call three times, followed by the boat's call letters, name, and position, and describe the trouble. You can also rapidly and repeatedly sound your horn, bell, or whistle. Fly your flag upside down. Blink your white range light or a spotlight using the standard SOS signal (three short blinks, three longer blinks, three short blinks). Fly an orange emergency signal flag (it shows an emblem of a black circle and square on it) or send up a flare.

The standard international radiotelephone distress call, "Mayday," comes from the French *m'aidez*, which means "help me.

Always wear a life jacket, or personal flotation device (PFD). The styles designed for Scout-age boaters can virtually guarantee that you will not drown as long as you are wearing one. This is simple, effective emergency prevention and preparedness.

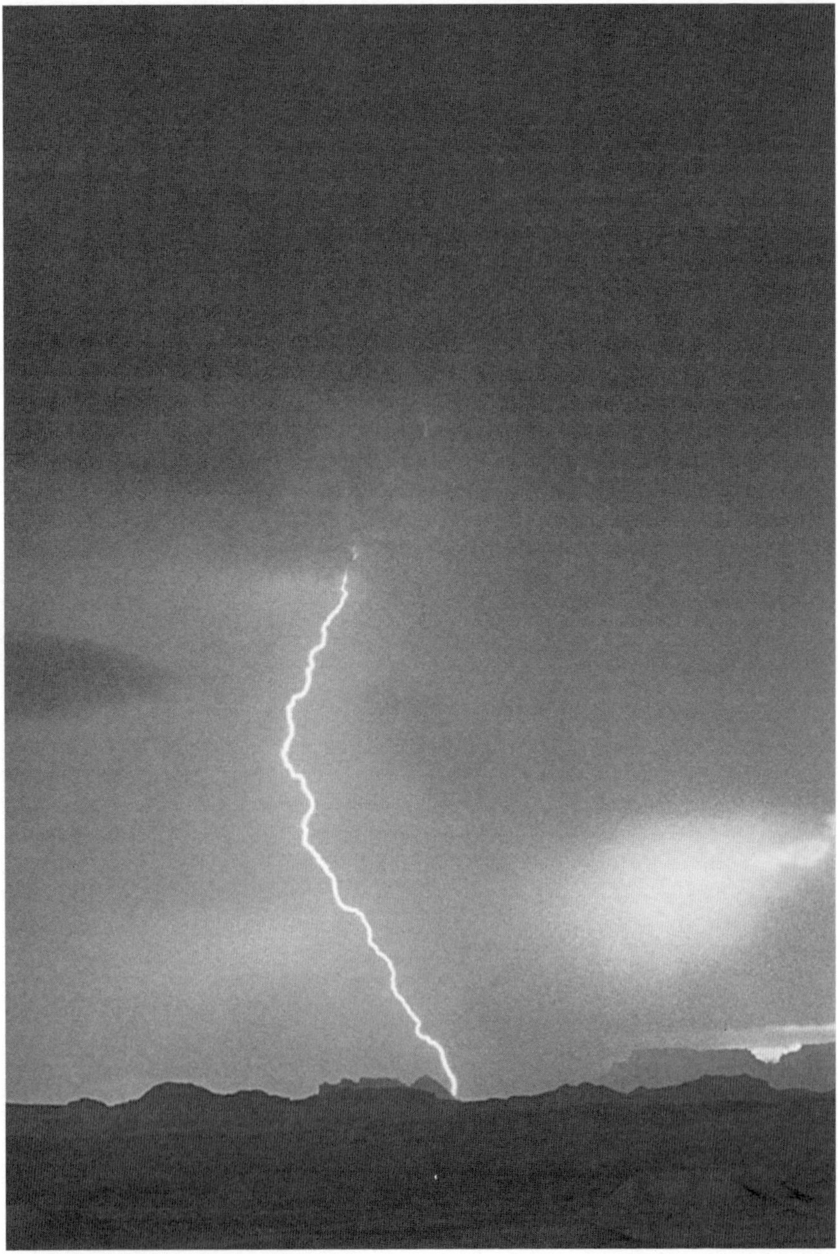

Weather-Related Emergencies

At the Storm Prediction Center in Norman, Oklahoma, meteorologists keep a careful eye on the nation's weather. The center
issues *watches* to local National Weather Service forecast
centers when severe weather is possible. When severe weather
or dangerous conditions are occurring, the local forecast office
issues *warnings*, which are announced on NOAA Weather
Radio as well as commercial radio and television. Watches and
warnings are issued for weather events such as winter storms,
tornadoes, severe thunderstorms, high winds, and flash floods.
Advisories also are issued when weather might cause serious
or dangerous conditions. A common advisory may alert
motorists to hazards such as slippery roads during wintry
weather, or boaters of rough water during high winds.

Meteorologists rely on weather radar to provide information
about developing storms. The National Weather Service has
installed Doppler radar stations throughout the country that
make it possible for them to issue life-saving warnings before
severe weather hits.

The National Oceanic and Atmospheric Administration (NOAA, pronounced
"Noah") runs NOAA Weather Radio, which is the only government-operated
radio system that provides warnings to the public about natural and
structural hazards. NOAA Weather Radio can be a lifesaver, and you can
be, too, by listening to it. For instance, during a deadly tornado outbreak
in Oklahoma and Kansas, a supervisor at a plant in Kansas saved more
than 100 people by responding to warnings issued by the National Weather
Service that he heard on the plant's NOAA Weather Radio. Shortly after he
told employees to move to the basement for safety, a tornado destroyed
the building. No one was hurt.

Flood

If you live along a river or any natural drainage system, flood can be a threat. Your family should learn the safest route from your home to high, safe ground in case you must leave your home (evacuate). Your local Red Cross chapter will be able to tell you about the history of flooding in your area. Find out whether your home is above or below flood stage level.

Flood watches and warnings are transmitted by radio, television, loudspeakers, and sirens. Know what the warning system is in your area. When a warning sounds, follow instructions. If you are told to evacuate, do so using recommended roads. Know your community flood evacuation plan.

Before a flood happens, you can do things to help reduce property loss and prevent injury to yourself and others. Store drinking water in as many containers as you can in case water

Floods can happen quickly. After a flood in Texas, one resident said, "About 11:00 last night the water started coming in over the bridge. Between 11:00 and 11:20 it was incredible how fast it rose. There was really no time to move. Or get out. Or anything. . . ."

service is cut off. You could even fill bathtubs and sinks. Have emergency supplies ready and get them to the highest inside part of your home. If you must evacuate, take these supplies with you.

During a flood watch, you can take other preventive measures—if you have time.

- Bring outside equipment indoors or tie it down. Garbage cans, lawn furniture, tools—anything that floats and can be carried along by floodwaters—can be a danger to others.

- Sandbags can help keep floodwaters from your home. But do not pile them up right against the foundation of the house; it is better if water can get into the cellar. This will equalize the water pressure inside and outside the foundation and help prevent damage to the foundation and the house.

- Unplug electrical appliances and equipment. Get your parents to turn off the gas running to gas appliances. If there is time, help them move furniture to high points in your home.

If you are caught in your home by rising waters, move to the second floor if you have one, and then to the roof, if necessary. Take your emergency supplies, including warm clothing, flashlights, and a battery-operated radio, and wait for help. Do not try to swim for safety. Rescue teams will be looking for you, and floodwaters can be deadly.

If you are advised to evacuate by car, do so immediately. If you wait, you could become trapped by flooded roads. Do not drive over flooded roads. Parts of the roadway might already be washed out. If your car stalls, abandon it. Floodwaters can rise rapidly and sweep away a car—and whoever is in it.

When floodwaters go down, throw away food, even canned goods, that came in contact with floodwaters because the water may have been contaminated. If your home has its own water well, have the water tested before anyone drinks it. Make sure anything electrical is completely dry before you use it.

Do not try to cross fast-moving water that is more than 6 inches deep. Fast-moving water is more powerful than you can imagine, and even 6 inches can knock you off your feet.

FEMA has a list of **disaster supplies** that it suggests that everyone have on hand:

- Flashlights and extra batteries
- Portable battery-operated radio and extra batteries
- First-aid kit and manual (or the *Boy Scout Handbook* or *First Aid* merit badge pamphlet)
- Emergency food (nonperishable) and water
- Nonelectric can opener
- Essential medicines
- Cash and credit cards
- Sturdy shoes

Tornado

Tornadoes can lift a house off of its foundation and throw cars up into the air. Even the most well-built home can be leveled. So recognition and prevention are very important aspects of tornado emergency preparedness. In some states, tornadoes happen every year. Find out how often they occur where you live.

Tornadoes happen most often between April and June. Be prepared by paying attention to the weather; know and look for the signs of severe weather and a potential tornado:

- Topsy-turvy clouds often appear, sometimes bulging downward instead of upward.
- It may rain heavily or hail before a tornado.
- Skies may take on a dark greenish color.
- Before a tornado hits, the wind may die and everything may become very still.

You might think that tornadoes happen only in the wide-open plains of Kansas or Oklahoma, but no place is safe from tornadoes. In the late 1980s a tornado swept through Yellowstone National Park and left a path of destruction up and down a 10,000-foot mountain.

Where Is Tornado Alley?

The central part of our country—from northern Minnesota and North Dakota to southern Texas and Louisiana—is sometimes called "Tornado Alley." Generally, this is the area where dangerous tornadoes are most likely to happen. However, these statistics vary. According to a map from FEMA, the number of tornadoes recorded per 1,000 square miles is highest in north Texas and central Oklahoma, with other danger spots in southern Missouri, Arkansas, Mississippi, and Alabama.

Everyone in your family should know the difference between a *tornado watch* and *tornado warning*. A watch means that tornadoes are possible and conditions are favorable for them to develop. A warning means that one has been sighted.

During a tornado warning, you and your family should move to your preplanned place of safety. At home, this should be in a basement or storm cellar, or a windowless, interior room (or even a closet) on the lowest floor of your home. Stay away from windows; windblown objects may break the glass. Take cover under a piece of heavy furniture and hold on to it. Cover yourself with blankets or pillows if you can.

If you live in a mobile home, do not stay there. Get out and find shelter.

If you live in an area that has a lot of tornadoes, your school will have plans for what to do during a tornado warning. The safest place is in an interior hallway on the lowest floor. Auditoriums, cafeterias, or gyms that have big, poorly supported roofs are not safe. This is good advice for any public place, too: Go to an interior hallway or restroom. Stay away from glass.

If you are in a car during a tornado warning, get out of the car and find shelter in a building. If there is no building or no time to get to one, lie flat in a nearby ditch, gully, or depression away from the car. Shield your head with your hands and arms. Never try to drive away from a tornado. They can do zigzags, figure eights, and U-turns—you might suddenly find yourself driving straight into one.

After a tornado, be prepared with your first-aid skills and your duty to *help other people.*

Hurricane

Anyone living along the Atlantic or Gulf coasts should be prepared for hurricanes. Atlantic hurricane season lasts from June 1 to November 30. During this time, listen to local weather reports and NOAA Weather Radio for hurricane progress reports. A hurricane *watch* is issued when there might be a hurricane within 24 to 36 hours. A *warning* is more serious and is issued when hurricane conditions (winds of 74 miles per hour or faster, and high water and rough seas) are expected in 24 hours or less. Plan with your family what to do during hurricane watches or warnings.

Take patio furniture, tools, trash cans, and loose lumber inside the house or tie them down. Have an adult shut off electricity and water. Leave natural gas service turned on because it may take many weeks for a professional to restore gas service after a major storm, and you may need gas for heating and cooking after the storm. Store a supply of safe

Pets and Disaster

Be prepared to protect your pets when disaster strikes. If you are a pet owner, include your pets in your family's disaster plan. If that includes plans for possible evacuation, plan to evacuate your pets, too. Leaving them behind, even if you think they are in a safe place, is likely to result in their being lost, injured, or worse.

- Have a safe place to take your pets. *Red Cross shelters cannot take pets because of health and safety regulations.* Check boarding facilities, animal shelters, friends and relatives, and even hotels and motels.

- Have a portable pet disaster supply kit that includes items such as medications, leashes or carriers, current photos in case your pet gets lost, food and water, bowls, bed, and toys.

For more information, contact The Humane Society, Disaster Services, 2100 L Street NW, Washington, DC 20037.

drinking water. Park your car in the garage or at least away from trees and poles.

If there is time, help your parents close and board up all the windows of your home. Do not leave any windows uncovered because the direction of hurricane winds changes as the storm passes overhead, threatening all sides of the home.

0300 UT AUGUST 19,

HURRICANE BOB

You might have to leave your home, especially if you live in a coastal area. If local emergency managers—by means of radio, television, or loudspeaker—advise people in your community to evacuate, go where you are told and travel only on roads they tell you to use. Government and disaster-relief agency officials will tell you where to get emergency housing and feeding.

If you are camping along or near a seashore when a hurricane watch is issued, immediately strike camp and leave the area.

Hurricanes are easily spotted by weather radar, as the weather pattern and clouds swirl into the recognizable "eye" of the storm.

Sometimes family members become separated during an emergency. Have a plan for getting the family back together. In case of fire in your home, that might be as simple as meeting outside by a big tree or in the neighbor's front yard. But for other disaster situations, FEMA suggests asking an out-of-state relative or friend to be the *family contact*. Everyone in your family should know that person's name, address, and phone number. It is often easier to call long distance after an emergency.

Hawaii is prone to natural disasters such as earthquakes and hurricanes.

Other Emergencies

Earthquake

Find out how earthquake-prone your area is and know how to be prepared.

When an earthquake strikes, stay calm. Do not run. If you are indoors, drop to the floor, cover yourself with something (such as blankets or pillows) for protection from falling glass and other objects, and hold on to something sturdy. Get beneath the nearest table, bench, desk, or other strong overhead support. If there is no sturdy furniture nearby, sit against an inside wall, preferably in the basement. Stay away from windows and outside doors. If other people are in the building and can hear you, shout instructions to them so that they know what to do, too.

Earthquakes can be felt in 39 states in the United States. They are felt most often on the West Coast and in Alaska and Hawaii, but they also can happen in the Midwest and in other areas.

If you are outdoors, stay there. Do not run near buildings. Head for the nearest vacant lot or the widest street. You should be out in the open where you will not get hit by falling wires, crumbling chimneys, or collapsing walls.

After tremors are over, if your parents are at home, get them to check for leaking gas. If you smell gas, open windows and doors and then get out of the house. Call the gas company from a neighbor's phone.

If you are in a car during an earthquake, the driver should pull off the road and park—but not under power lines or wires. Stay in the car until tremors are over. When you continue, drive slowly and help the driver watch for fallen objects, downed power lines, and broken and otherwise dangerous roadways.

Aftershocks are smaller quakes that can occur in the hours, days, and weeks after a larger earthquake. Be prepared for them as for an earthquake. They can be strong enough to knock down anything that the main tremors may have weakened.

Food-Borne Disease

If you eat food or drink beverages that are contaminated with any number of bacteria, toxins, or parasites, you could get a food-borne disease, or food poisoning. Common symptoms are nausea, vomiting, abdominal cramps, and diarrhea. About 250 different food-borne diseases have been described; it can be a big problem, but recognizing where and how the problem might occur and taking some simple precautions can go a long way in avoiding an emergency situation.

The Centers for Disease Control and Prevention suggests five simple precautions that you can take to help reduce the risk of getting a food-borne disease:

- **Cook** food thoroughly, particularly meat, poultry, and eggs.

- **Separate** your food to avoid *cross-contamination*, or bacteria moving from one food or place to another. Wash your hands after you touch raw meat; wash utensils and cutting boards, too. Store food separately.

- **Chill** leftovers right away. Bacteria grows quickly at room temperature. Keep cold cuts, meat, and dairy products covered and refrigerated. If any food has been left in an open container and unrefrigerated for a long time, do not use it.

Cooking that food and/or chilling it will not make it safe to eat.

- **Clean** fruits and vegetables thoroughly under running water. Wash your hands with soap and water before handling food.

- **Report** any suspected food-borne illness to your local health department. If agencies designed to help in emergency situations do not know about when and how such situations arise, they will not be able to develop ways to prevent future emergencies.

Botulism, caused by a toxin secreted from a bacterium, is the most serious form of food poisoning. People usually become infected by eating home-preserved food that was not properly washed and preserved. Throw away any foods you think might be spoiled. If you find yourself in an emergency situation and you must eat home-canned food that may be spoiled, boil the food for at least 15 minutes, which will make the toxin completely inactive.

Food and Camping

Campers can easily get food-borne diseases—and having cramps, nausea, or diarrhea when you are in the wilderness is not something anyone wants. Here are some tips for safe camp food practices:

- Plan meals so that you do not have any leftovers; if you do have leftovers, do not eat them. Throw them away or pack them out.

- Plan meals that require as little chilled food as possible. If you do have a camp cooler, do not "stretch" the ice—get more when you need it so food stays cold enough.

- If food has been at room temperature for more than two hours, do not eat it.

- Be absolutely certain that any edible foods you collect near camp are safe to eat. With many plants, such as mushrooms, only trained experts can identify which ones are safe.

Nuclear Power Plant Emergency

As we moved into the new millennium in 2000, about 100 nuclear power plants were operating in the United States. No one has ever been killed by an accident at one of these plants, but in 1986, 30 people died during an emergency at the Chernobyl plant in Russia (then the Soviet Union), and more than 100,000 people were evacuated. During an emergency at a nuclear facility, radiation can be released that is dangerous to people near the plant.

State and local governments have preparedness plans for areas in a 10-mile radius and 50-mile radius from all nuclear power plants. You can get emergency information from the power company that operates the plant or from the local office of emergency management. You and your family should have and be familiar with this information.

The worst nuclear emergency in the United States happened in 1979 at the Three Mile Island nuclear power plant in Pennsylvania. No one was hurt, but as a result of what officials learned during that emergency, nuclear plants are even safer today.

You also can become familiar with the warning systems that will be in place. These could include sirens, alerts on radios, or *route alerting* (like Paul Revere) to notify the public. If sirens are used in your area, find out when they will be tested so that you can hear what they sound like and how well you can hear them from your home. (This also is good advice for warning sirens used for other emergencies such as tornadoes or dangerous thunderstorms.)

Learn about the emergency plans at places where your family members might be, such as schools, child care centers, and nursing homes. Learn where people are supposed to go if there is an evacuation. Be prepared to evacuate with emergency supplies, as you might be for another emergency.

There are four levels of emergency at nuclear power plants:

- A **notification of an unusual event** is the least serious. Something unusual or unexpected has happened at the plant, but the public does not have to do anything special. Emergency officials are notified.

- An **alert** means that something has happened to reduce plant safety, but all the backup systems are still working and no one is in danger.

- A **site area emergency** is more serious. Small amounts of radiation might be released into the air or water, but these levels are still expected to be safe outside the boundaries of the plant.

- A **general emergency** is the most serious problem. Radiation could leak outside the plant and off the plant site. Sirens will be sounded or other alert systems used. You should listen to the radio and watch television. Local authorities will provide information and instructions. Follow their instructions promptly—you may be advised to evacuate or take shelter.

If you are told to stay indoors, close doors, windows, and chimney dampers. You want to keep outside air from getting in. Turn off forced-air heating or air-conditioning. Put food in covered containers or in the refrigerator. If you can, go to the basement or another underground area. Stay there until you are told it is safe to leave. Do not use the telephone unless absolutely necessary; all lines will be needed for emergency calls.

If you are told to evacuate, stay calm. You will have plenty of time to leave. When outdoors, cover your nose and mouth with a handkerchief. When you go back indoors, change your clothes and shower. Put the clothes you were wearing in a plastic bag and seal it. When you leave your home, lock the doors and windows. Keep car windows and vents closed. Listen to the radio for updates, evacuation routes, and other instructions. Review the emergency information you got from the power company, which will include a map of evacuation routes and where you can find relocation centers.

Most radioactivity loses its strength fairly quickly. Authorities will monitor radiation release and will let the public know when any danger has passed.

Emergency in a Public Place

It seems that we hear about emergencies in public places more and more—in schools, office buildings, shopping malls, and restaurants, and even in churches. As in your home, recognizing potential emergency situations is the first step in preparedness. In your school, for instance, do you see any fire hazards in the building? Are conditions and practices in shops, labs, and the

As much as possible, be prepared *before* trouble strikes in public. For instance, get into the habit of looking for exits in any public building you enter.

gym safe? Are the waste collection, storage, and disposal practices safe? If you see any unsafe conditions in your school, tell a teacher, the principal, or another adult you can talk to.

One important thing you can always do when facing any emergency is to *stay calm* and as clear-headed as you can. In a public place, this can be especially important because there may be other people around you who are afraid and not acting in a safe manner. You may have heard the story of someone yelling "Fire!" in a crowded theater. The audience members all react at once, rushing for a door as they try to escape. Such sudden, unthinking reactions can cause more serious accidents, and even death, so learn how to control your own fear. Try not to give in to it, as it can cloud your judgment. If you are calm, you may be able to help other people stay calm. Set an example.

Always remember that you must never endanger yourself when you are facing an emergency. A violent situation in public, for instance, may be very dangerous. If you can safely do so, call for help. Otherwise, sometimes the wisest thing you can do is to protect yourself and wait for help to come to you.

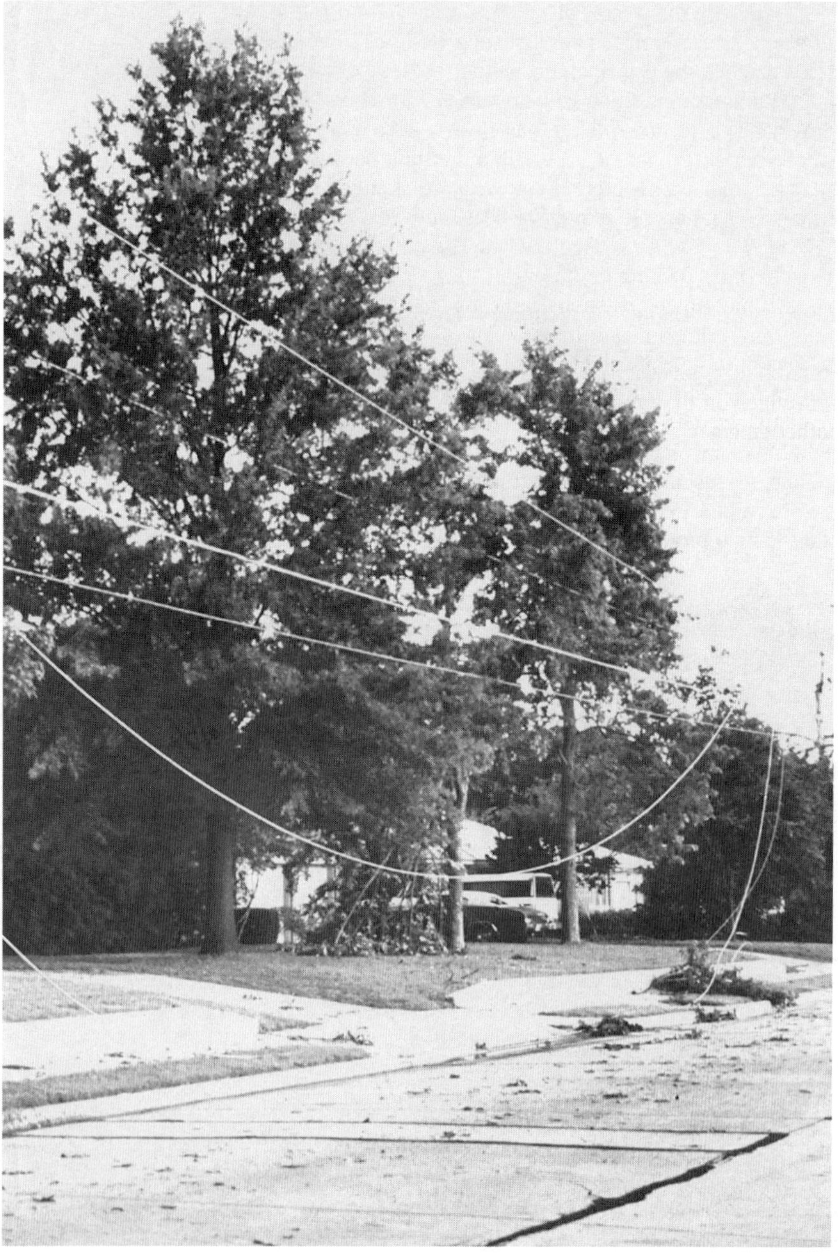

Saving Lives

After an emergency, your reaction may save lives. You can save lives with your knowledge of first aid and your knowledge of situations that might be dangerous. Earning the Lifesaving merit badge, for instance, will prepare you to react safely and effectively in the event of water emergencies. Here are some other emergency situations.

Contact With a Live Wire

Electrical appliances usually are safe, but eventually, wires fray, plugs break, and parts loosen. Furthermore, circuits in your home might be overloaded with too many extension cords and appliances.

It is extremely dangerous to touch a "live" wire—that is, a wire that has electrical current running through it. If someone grabs a bare spot on a live wire, he or she might not be able to let go. Call for help. Pull the plug or cord, grabbing it only where it is well-insulated. Or, get to the main electrical switch in your home and shut off the power.

If you can't shut off the power, try to push the wire away with a dry, wooden stick (like a broom handle) or a rolled-up newspaper, which does not conduct electricity. If that doesn't work, you can separate the victim from the wire. But make sure you are not standing on a wet surface. Water is an excellent conductor of electricity. If possible, put on heavy, dry gloves before trying the rescue. Otherwise, you can use a dry handkerchief, towel, sheet, or other dry cloth to encircle the wire and pull the wire from the victim's hand. *Do not touch the wire, the victim, or any grounded object such as water pipes.*

Once you separate someone from a live wire, call an ambulance or paramedics.

Rescuing a person
who has come
into contact with
a live power
line outdoors
is extremely
dangerous. A
Scout should not
try such a rescue.
Call 9-1-1 or the
fire department.

Windstorms, rain, ice, and snowstorms can down power lines and plunge towns into darkness. If you see a power line down outdoors, call the electric company, police, or fire department so that they can shut off the power immediately. Stay nearby to warn others of the danger, but *stay away from the power line.*

The *Electricity* merit badge pamphlet has more information about electric shock, accident prevention, and rescue techniques that will help you be prepared for electrical emergencies.

Carbon Monoxide Poisoning

Carbon monoxide (CO) is an odorless and colorless gas—and it can kill. Every year in the United States, CO poisoning kills more than 200 people and sends thousands more to the hospital.

Carbon monoxide gas can come from a lot of places: gas-fired appliances, charcoal grills, wood-burning furnaces or fireplaces, and cars. Running a car in a closed garage, for instance, is a recipe for disaster.

Everyone is at risk for CO poisoning, but you can do some simple things to prevent a problem:

• Install a CO alarm in your home.

• Make sure your parents have any fuel-burning appliances, furnaces, and chimneys inspected by a professional at least once a year.

• Never use a charcoal grill in the garage or in your home— only outdoors!

Know the symptoms of CO poisoning: headache, dizziness, faintness, and ringing in the ears. A person might yawn a lot or feel like vomiting. If you or someone else feels like this, get outside or open windows right away for fresh air.

If someone is overcome by CO poisoning, call for medical help. The person may not be able to breathe. Give rescue breathing as you learned to do for the First Aid merit badge. Make sure that all appliances and sources of combustion are turned off. A professional should investigate the source of the CO buildup and repair it.

Clothes on Fire

Accidents involving burning clothes are the second greatest cause of serious burns. If your clothes catch fire, remember "Stop, drop, and roll." Running will merely fan the flames and cause them to burn more. Try to keep calm. Stop where you are and drop to the ground. Roll over and over to smother the flames. Cover your face with your hands.

You can use this technique if someone else's clothes catch fire, too. Knock the person over, tackle or trip the person, and then roll him or her over and over several times. If you can, grab a rug, coat, jacket, or blanket to wrap around him or her and help smother the flames. But do not waste time running off to look for something.

After the fire is out, cold water will help cool the skin and reduce damage from burning. Call for medical help as soon as possible.

The rule for clothes on fire, whether yours or someone else's, is "Stop, drop, and roll."

Drowning

If you know the rescue methods *reach*, *throw*, and *row*, you might be able to save a *drowning* person—and avoid drowning, yourself, during the rescue. These are *nonswimming* methods of rescue.

- **Reach** with anything you can: your leg or arm, a broom, a branch, a paddle, a pole. Lying down on or otherwise bracing yourself from a dock or solid ground, reach to the victim with something he or she can grab onto. Pull the person to shore. You can lengthen your reach by wading into the water or by holding onto a dock or another firmly anchored object.

REACH

- **Throw** help to a victim if the person is out of reach. You may find ring buoys attached to a line ready for use at most protected beaches and pools. A throwing rescue does not have to involve something with a line attached to it. Anything that floats well enough to support someone will help—life jackets and flotation cushions, inner tubes, air mattresses, kickboards, empty water jugs, and even coolers.

THROW

- **Row** to a person in trouble if you can't reach or throw. When you get near the victim, row backward to him or her and take the person aboard over the back end of the boat. Or if you have a buddy with you, your buddy can hold onto the victim while you tow the person ashore (but only do this if you are not far from shore and the victim is not injured).

Use a boat with an outboard motor if you can, especially if the victim is far from shore. Stop the motor as you get near the victim, and then reach out with a paddle or pole.

If a canoe is the only craft handy, use it. Sit on the bottom in the center. Paddle on the side nearest the victim and use the paddle to steady the canoe as the victim climbs in over the side. If you overturn, get the victim to hang onto the canoe. Swim to one end and, with a strong kick, push the canoe back to shore. In a tight spot, you also can use a surfboard, paddle-board, or air mattress in the same way.

ROW

Throwing Lines

An essential skill in a water emergency is the ability to throw a line smoothly and accurately: Practice first so that you can throw it accurately.

With a light line, tie a bowline in the shore end of the line; pass the loop through it to form a running knot. Loop this around your left wrist to anchor the shore end when you throw. With a heavy line, you might have to tie a knot in the shore end and step on it or tie it down.

Carefully coil a light line to form smooth loops in your left hand. Split the coil and hold half in each hand to make throwing underhand easier and more accurate.

Also throw a ring buoy underhand. Don't divide the coil—the extra weight improves accuracy. Hold the buoy in your throwing hand and the coiled line in your other hand.

Throw the ring buoy to land *beyond* the victim and the attached line will rest over his or her shoulder or within easy reach. The victim can grab either the rope or the ring buoy as you pull him or her to safety.

Quickly retrieve and coil the line for another throw if needed. If you are right-handed, throw with your left foot forward and right foot back. To retrieve the line, drop your left hand in position for holding the coil as you pull in the line with your right hand. Save time by keeping your feet firmly planted in the same position when throwing and pulling in the line.

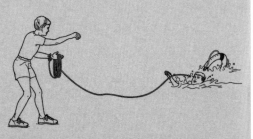

For heavy line, use these same procedures. If you can't coil the line in your left hand, or if it is too heavy to hold, coil it neatly on the ground. Step on the shore end of the line or tie it down. Hold only the portion that you can grasp comfortably in your right hand and throw it toward your target.

Ice Rescue

Reach, *throw*, and *go* are ice-rescue methods. If you see someone fall through ice, act quickly but think clearly. Decide on the best rescue method.

- **Reach.** If you can't reach out from shore and pull the person in, you might be able to reach out to the person with a pole, tree branch, oar, or ladder—anything that will reach. Push it over the ice so that the person can grab it.

- **Throw.** Throw a rope to the person if you can. Put a loop (bowline) in the end of the rope so the victim can slip it over himself or herself if necessary. The person's hands might be too cold to hang on. If you have a ring buoy tied to the end of a heaving line, slide it across the ice to the victim.

- **Go.** If you can't reach or throw, go—but *carefully.* Spread-eagle over the ice and wiggle your way to the person. Once you get closer, reach to them with something long. You want to go out on the ice as *little* as possible.

After you rescue someone from ice water, get them indoors right away. *Hypothermia*—or the lowering of the body's temperature to dangerous levels—can be another emergency. Remove the person's wet clothes. Rub him or her down with a dry towel; wrap the victim in blankets. Give the person something warm to drink. For more information on the symptoms and treatment of hypothermia, see the *First Aid* merit badge pamphlet.

A "human chain" on ice can save a life. Snake out onto the ice while someone holds your ankles. Someone else holds that person's ankles. Build your chain, hands-on-ankles, until you reach the victim.

Lowering a Person Using a Commercial Harness

Mountain rescue teams may have to lower an injured person from a cliff or down rock faces. A firefighter may have to lower someone from a window of a burning building. A commercial harness, such as those that climbers and rappellers use, also can be used in emergency rescue work. Many Scouting activities use harnesses that can be self-tied, but for safety's sake during an emergency rescue, it is recommended to use a commercial harness and carefully follow the manufacturer's instructions.

If a person is conscious and not badly injured, he or she can hold onto the rope as you pay it out. As you do so, turn the rope around a firmly anchored object such as a tree or large boulder. The person being lowered can use his or her feet to keep from banging into anything on the way down. Work out the rope hand over hand. If you let it slide through your hands, you could burn them badly, lose control of the rope, and drop the person.

Lowering an unconscious or severely injured person is more difficult. You should try it only if you have had special training or if you are working with an expert.

Rope rescue is a challenging activity, especially in remote areas. Techniques and equipment are constantly being revised. If you are in a rope rescue situation, you should work with a trained expert.

Long-Distance Moving

The unexpected can happen anywhere—and sometimes far from help. You may need to transport an injured person for a long distance—and save a life by doing it.

When you are moving an injured person, no matter what method you are using, make sure you rest enough so that you do not become a second casualty. If just you and a buddy are doing the transporting, stop every 30 to 60 minutes and rest 5 to 10 minutes. How often you stop will depend on how much the victim weighs and how rugged the terrain is.

FOUR-HANDED SEAT CARRY

Two first-aiders can transport a conscious person with this carry. Each bearer grasps his own right wrist with his left hand. The two bearers then lock hands with each other. The patient sits on their hands and places his arms around their shoulders.

TWO-PERSON CARRY

The bearers kneel on either side of the victim. Each bearer slides one arm under the victim's back and one under his thighs. The bearers grasp each other's wrists, then rise from the ground with the patient supported between them.

If you must carry an injured person for a long way, make a litter or stretcher. You will need two strong poles, branches, or small straight trees 4 to 6 feet long and a blanket, tarp, jacket, or sleeping bag. To make a sleeping bag litter, slip the two poles inside the bag and cut them so that they are a foot longer than the bag. Or, you can use two shirts for the litter.

Test the litter's strength before you try to carry anyone on it. Carry the person feetfirst unless you have to go uphill, and then carry him or her headfirst. Keep the litter as level as you can.

If the injured person is conscious and you do not have a way to make a litter, use the four-handed seat.

When carrying someone else, this good advice for hiking outdoors is even more important: Never step on anything you can step over, and never step over anything you can step around.

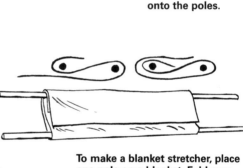

Two shirts and two poles will make a strong stretcher. Button all the buttons and then turn the shirts inside out onto the poles.

To make a blanket stretcher, place one pole on a blanket. Fold over two-fifths of the blanket. Place the second pole 6 inches from the edge of the folded-over part. Bring the edge of the blanket over the pole. Fold over the remaining part of the blanket. The person's weight will keep the blanket from unfolding.

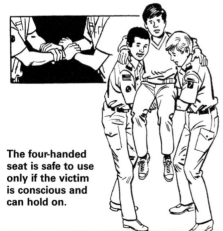

The four-handed seat is safe to use only if the victim is conscious and can hold on.

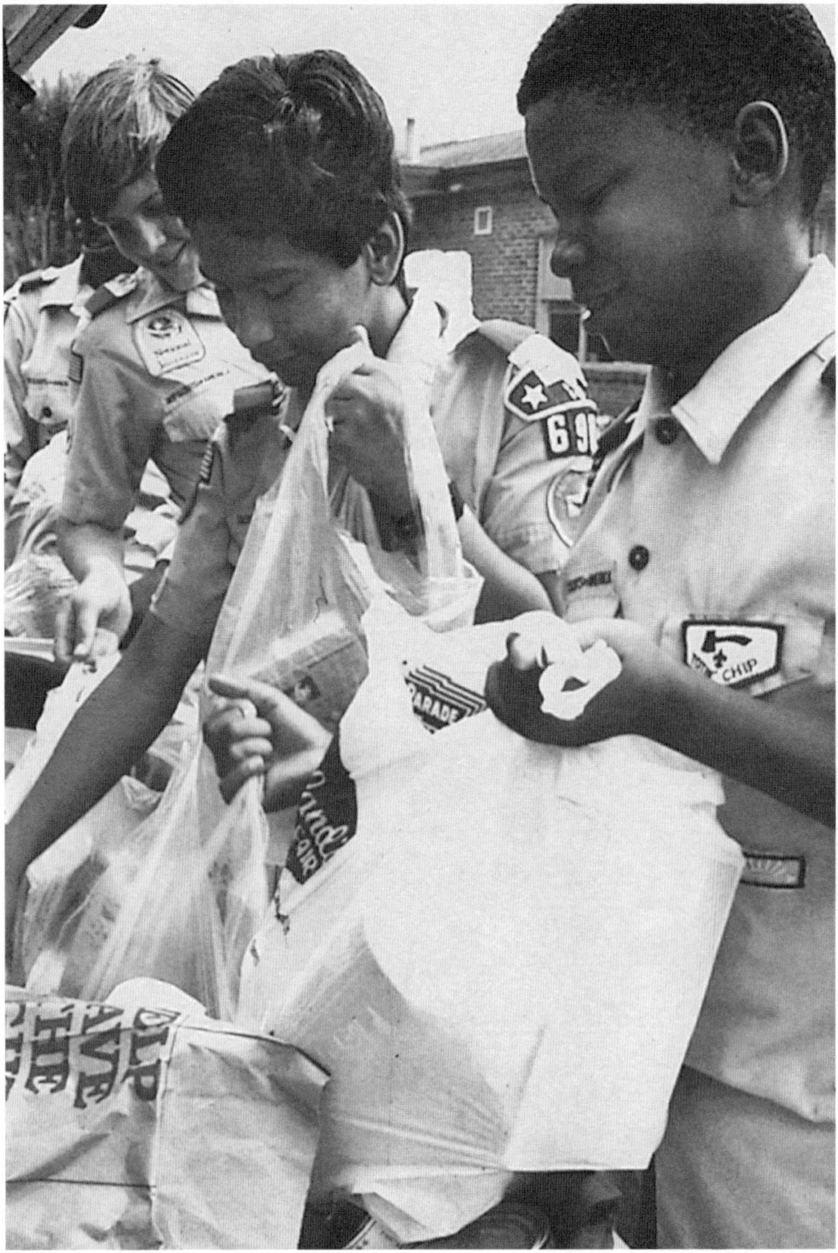
PARADE
CHIP

Community Emergency Service

For as long as there has been Scouting, Scouts have provided outstanding services in emergencies of all kinds. You can learn about emergency preparedness. You can learn to recognize, prevent, and react to emergency situations. But carrying out emergency service work is the best training of all.

As a Scout, you know about living outdoors, camping, cooking, first aid, and how to make a shelter. With knowledge like this, you and your troop can be prepared for emergency service in your community.

Crowd and Traffic Control

Scout troops in the past have helped police and fire departments, emergency management officials, and the Red Cross handle crowd and traffic control. Today, it is felt that Scouts should do this only at official Boy Scouts of America functions. In any case, crowd and traffic control *must* be done under the supervision of officials in charge of the situation.

Each member of a crowd-control crew needs a staff about 2 inches in diameter and 6 feet long. To move a crowd back, crew members hold the staffs horizontally at chest height and advance slowly toward the crowd. To keep the crowd back, form a chain with your staffs. To direct the movement of a crowd, indicate direction by pointing or blocking the way.

During daylight hours, a fluorescent or reflective vest should be worn. After dark, every member of a crowd-control crew should wear a reflective vest or high-visibility material on the right ankle and arm.

Messenger Service and Communications

Providing messenger service during an emergency takes planning. Your BSA local council, along with other community organizations, will assign a service area to your troop—usually one that is near your meeting place. Your troop should make a large-scale map of the area and assign sections to each patrol. Each patrol then prepares its own sectional map and learns it inside out. Get to know shortcuts, easiest routes, dead-end streets, traffic blocks, trails, even cow paths—anything that will help you get from one point to another during an emergency.

Bikes can speed up delivery but must be in top condition for a reliable messenger service. Cyclers also must know and practice bicycle safety at all times (see the *Cycling* merit badge pamphlet). In some areas, older Scouts and leaders may deliver messages by car, snowmobile, boat, horse, or skis.

During emergencies, each messenger should carry a flashlight, personal first-aid kit, pencil, paper, map, pocketknife, and money. After delivering a written message, get a written receipt and return it with any answer to the sender.

Scouts might deliver messages within a control center during emergencies, freeing adults for other work. Troops also can help with communications. If telephones are working, Scouts can act as operators, taking incoming calls and relaying information to officials in charge. If phones don't work, signal teams might be set up, with four Scouts to a team. One Scout acts as team chief and observer, another as the signaler, the third as the recorder, and the fourth as the messenger. Messages are sent by Morse code using signal flags, signal lamps, blinkers, or flashlights or by semaphore or hand signaling.

Some Scouts and leaders specialize in radio communications. Some are qualified as amateur radio operators, Radio Amateur Civil Emergency Service (RACES) operators for emergency situations, or citizens band (CB) operators. CB units can consult and coordinate with local emergency management organizations such as the Red Cross and can serve as a primary means of communication.

> The Radio Amateur Civil Emergency Service (RACES) was founded in 1952 as a public service that provides volunteer communications within government agencies during times of extraordinary need. Each period of RACES activation is different, but the common thread is communications. You can learn more at their Web site: *http://www.races.net.*

Collection and Distribution Services

During and after some disasters, such as floods and tornadoes, many people may be without food and clothing. People may be homeless for a time. Scout troops working under the direction of their leaders and local officials can help collect needed items and get them to a central distribution point. Usually, officials will set up collection and distribution points at places such as churches, fire stations, schools, and other public buildings. Your troop meeting place might be used.

If your troop has developed a master map of your community, you will know where food stores are. This will save time in rounding up supplies. Scouts also can distribute leaflets or instructions for the Red Cross, the local emergency management agency, or other local authorities and volunteer groups.

Many Scouting units already know about and have experience collecting and distributing food through their work in the Scouting for Food National Good Turn.

Mass Feeding, Shelter, and Sanitation

The San Francisco Bay Area Council once recruited Scout troops to help the Red Cross feed 250 people during an emergency. Before the Red Cross could move in its "big" equipment, the Scouts arrived. Within three hours of the first mobilization signal, each Scout patrol had enough water boiling in improvised 5-gallon-can cookpots to make and serve hot soup and coffee.

If your troop is prepared with cooking cans (four per patrol), grates and grills, trench shovels, axes, Scout staves, firestarters, twine or rope (to mark off serving areas), and a fuel supply (such as charcoal), you will be prepared for mass feeding during an emergency.

Always coordinate activities with the Red Cross or local authorities. Under the direction of the officials in charge, Scouts could properly set up tents in designated areas. Troop tents or family camping tents could be used.

Scouts know more about emergency sanitation than most people. Troops can help treat water if clean water service is not available after an emergency. Wherever an emergency shelter has been set up, emergency sanitation often must be provided. Troops also can round up covered containers for garbage or come up with other possibilities for dealing with trash.

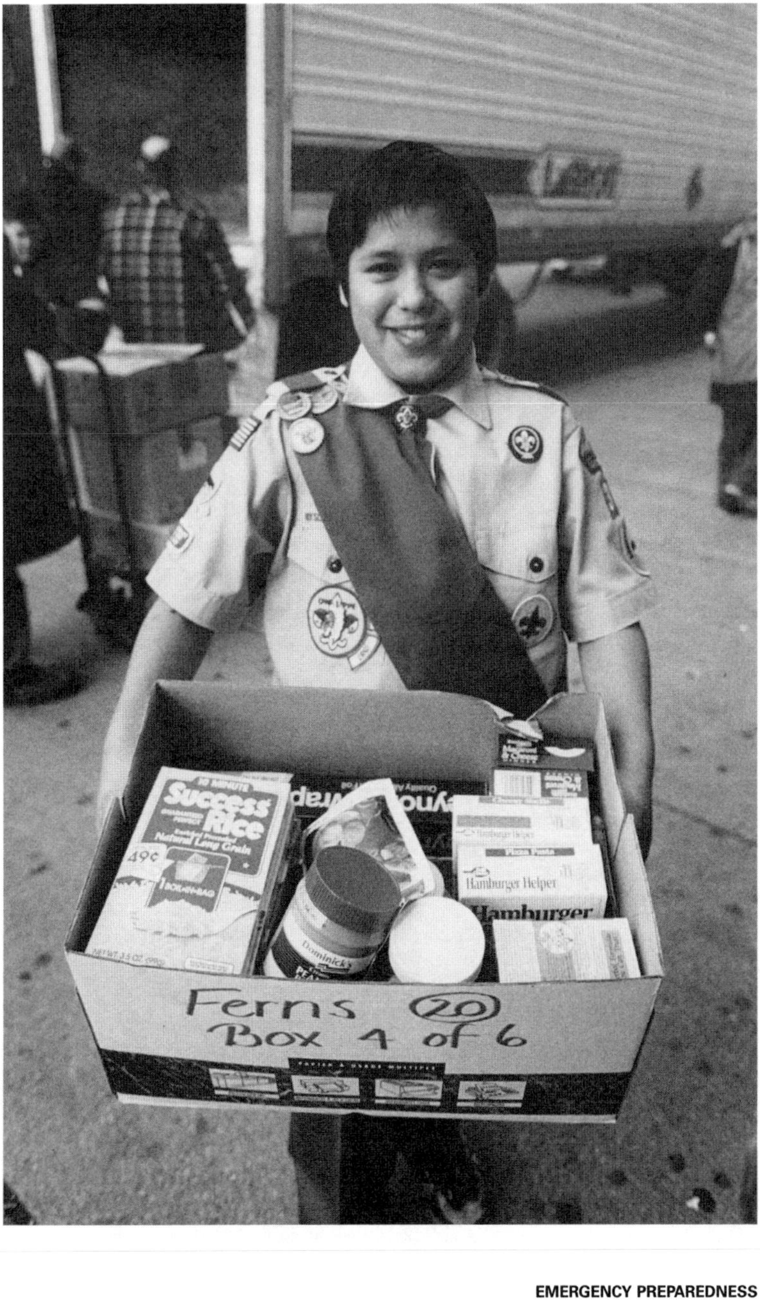
Success Rice
Natural Long Grain
49¢
Hamburger Helper
Pizza Pasta
Hamburger Helper
Hamburger
Ferns 20
Box 4 of 6

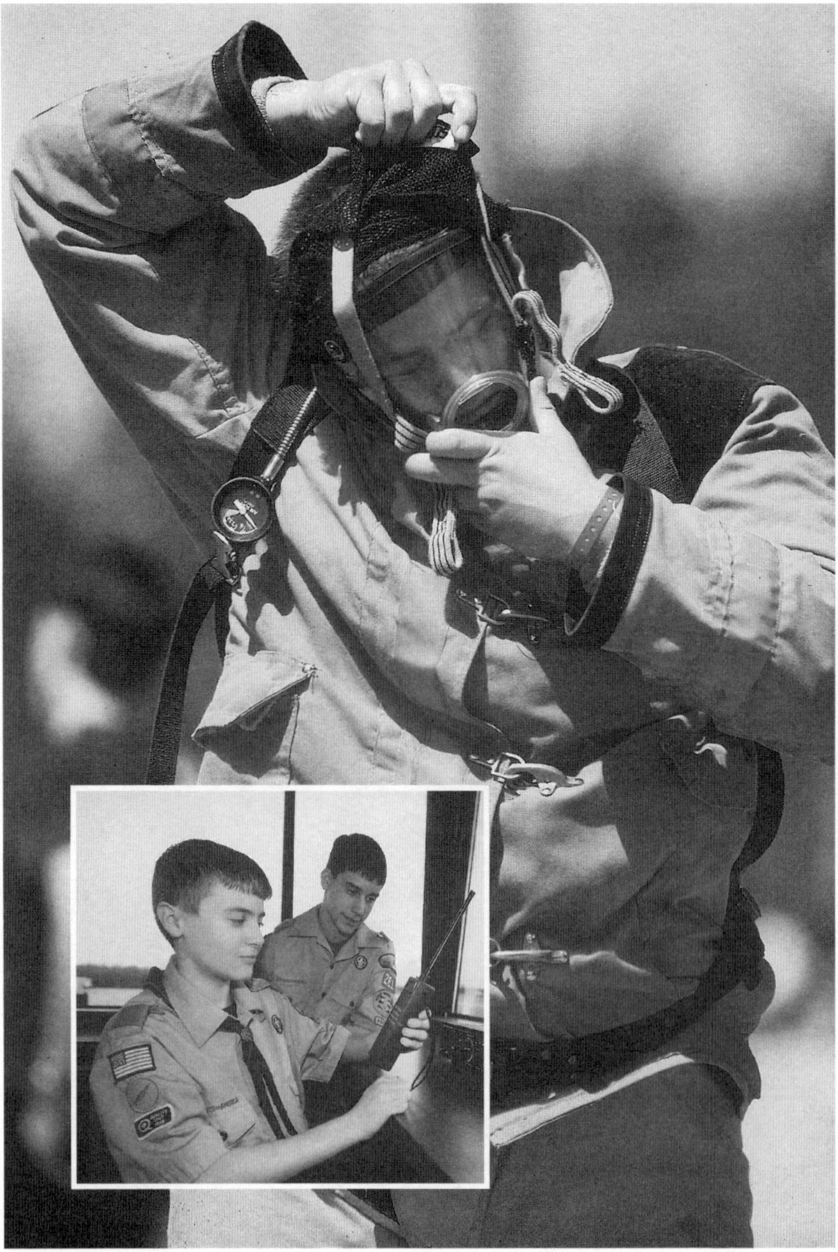

Emergency Mobilization Plans and Preparation

Is your troop prepared with a mobilization plan if your community asks you to help during an emergency? In any disaster, your first responsibility is to your family and home. But if a tornado has hit a neighboring town, or a nearby community is threatened with a flood or other emergency situation, your troop might be called upon to help.

You will be asked to be at a specific place at a specific time. If the telephones are working, use mobilization plan B; if phone lines are down, your troop must use mobilization plan A. Your troop should be prepared to use both plans.

If your troop has never set up a mobilization plan, discuss it with your Scoutmaster. Every community needs one. Any emergency plan for community service should be worked out by your Scoutmaster with the director of the local office of emergency management or with a disaster/emergency response coordinator in your area. If your community does not have

an emergency management or civil defense office, your Scoutmaster should check with the local American Red Cross chapter or the police or fire department. These officials can advise how your troop can help in an emergency.

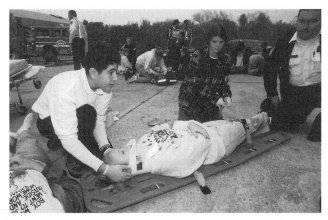

Mobilization Plans

Use **Plan A** when normal communications systems are unavailable. This plan involves planning and making contacts on the basis of *proximity*, or nearness. Leaders and Scouts make personal contact with troop members living near them. A Scoutmaster may first learn of the need for the troop's services when a police car or other emergency vehicle drives to the Scoutmaster's home with

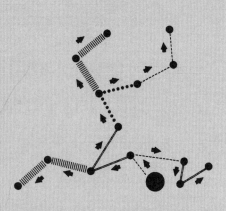

an authorized and approved request for the troop's services. Under this plan, the Scoutmaster goes to the home of a member in one direction from the Scoutmaster's home, and then to the home of a member in another direction. In a similar manner, each Scout personally contacts two members of the troop. This process continues until all have been notified of the mobilization call and the group is en route to the assembly point.

Use **Plan B** when normal phone communications are available. Troops mobilize by patrols. Members are contacted by phone. To begin

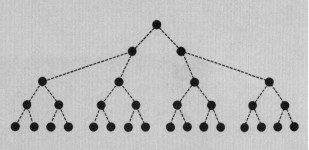

the mobilization, the Scoutmaster calls the assistant Scoutmaster and the senior patrol leader. They each phone two patrol leaders. Each patrol leader phones two patrol members. This procedures continues through the entire troop roster. The word is passed from person to person. If a member can't be reached, contact must be assumed by the caller.

Personal Emergency Service Pack

Be prepared for a mobilization call with a personal emergency service pack. You will be ready for many emergencies if you use the following checklist as you equip your pack:

☐ Poncho or raincoat (with hood, hat, or sou'wester)

☐ Change of underwear and socks

☐ Small bag with toothbrush, toothpaste, soap, comb, needle, thread, shoelaces, and toilet paper

☐ Sleeping bag (or bedroll of two wool blankets) and waterproof ground cloth

☐ Maps of areas where your troop is likely to serve

☐ 50 feet of No. 5 sash cord or similar-size nylon cord

☐ Hand ax or belt knife

☐ Water filtration equipment

☐ Cook kit and canteen

☐ Flashlight

☐ Battery-powered radio

☐ Extra batteries (stored separately)

☐ Hard hat

☐ Other equipment as determined by weather conditions (winter jacket, rubber boots, gloves, etc.)

☐ Personal first-aid kit (You can order a personal first-aid kit through your local council service center, or you can make your own. Include gauze bandages and pads, adhesive bandages, soap, antibiotic ointment for burns, and roller bandages.)

☐ Matches in a waterproof container

☐ Emergency ration (well-wrapped)

☐ Pencil and small notebook

☐ Handkerchief

☐ Compass

☐ Watch (unless you usually wear one)

☐ Facial tissues

☐ Work gloves

Family Emergency Kit

If you have received a warning that requires you and your family to evacuate your home, you might have time to throw together a few items or dash to a well-stocked emergency shelter. It would be better to have a box or suitcase of supplies ready. A prepared family keeps enough emergency supplies on hand to meet its needs for a few days or, better, for a week. These items come in handy in an emergency even if you do not have to evacuate. Some families keep their supplies in a basement shelter area or in a storm cellar, if they have one.

Include the following items:

☐ Three-day supply of water (1 gallon per person per day) stored in sealed, unbreakable containers such as plastic jugs

☐ Nonperishable packaged or canned food and a nonelectric can opener

☐ Eating utensils

☐ Any special foods or other items for babies, elderly people, or family members with disabilities

☐ Family first-aid kit

☐ Prescription medications (Make sure, however, that all medications are kept up-to-date; check their expiration dates regularly.)

☐ Battery-powered radio

☐ Flashlight or lantern

☐ Extra batteries (stored separately and rotated regularly)

☐ Matches in waterproof container

☐ Blankets or a sleeping bag for each family member

☐ Emergency toilet, if needed (Use a garbage container, bucket, or similar watertight container with a snug-fitting lid; plastic bags for liners; and household disinfectant such as chlorine bleach for odor control.)

Major Disaster Preparedness Items

The above list is useful if you have to leave your home. The following items are also helpful during an emergency or if you are staying in your home after one.

☐ List of emergency telephone numbers (In your area, 9-1-1 may be the only number needed for any emergency.)

☐ Fire extinguisher

☐ Tool kit, including ax, shovel, broom, screwdriver, pliers, hammer, coil of half-inch rope, coil of baling wire, plastic or duct tape, razor blades, adjustable wrench for turning off gas or water

☐ Simple chart showing where shutoff valves are located, including the main electrical switch

☐ Portable fire escape ladder for homes or buildings of more than one level

☐ Portable stove that uses butane or charcoal (used outdoors to avoid the danger of carbon monoxide poisoning)

☐ Gloves and cloths for cleaning up chemical spills

☐ Covered containers (that can be tightly sealed) for storing refuse

☐ Garden hose kept near an outside faucet at all times

Getting Involved: Emergency Service Projects

To meet the emergency service project requirement for the Emergency Preparedness merit badge, you must take an active role. Merely being at an emergency isn't enough. The part you play must be one that you have been trained for (or trained yourself for). You may participate in an emergency service project during a real emergency, but normally you will have to perform a practice drill with your troop or a local community service organization.

You can help your troop plan and conduct an activity that involves an emergency service project. A practice mobilization may be a part of the project but will not qualify as your emergency service project. Your Scoutmaster and troop might consider one of the following activities.

The American Red Cross is a humanitarian organization associated with the International Red Cross Movement that provides relief to victims of disasters and helps people prevent, prepare for, and respond to emergencies. You or your Scoutmaster might contact your local Red Cross chapter to find out how you might get involved in emergency service projects.

Lost-Child Project

Scouts often are called upon to help find people who are lost, and they need to know how to do it. You can help train your troop with a lost-child project.

Usually, Scouts are called together through a troop mobilization plan. The plan is organized with the patrol leader to set it into action. Be sure to announce the equipment needed for the activity, either before or at the time of the mobilization call.

For the project, make one or more "lost child" dummies from burlap sacks stuffed with straw or hay. Put a shirt on the lost child so that searchers will recognize it. Before the mobilization call, place the dummy somewhere in the search territory. Position it in an area that will prove challenging and interesting to searchers. To test the searchers' powers of observation, plant some barely noticeable "evidence" (such as clothing or footprints) of the lost child.

After Scouts have been assembled by the mobilization call, organize them into search parties and use the lost-person search method. Be sure patrols have practiced. Mark the search area on maps that are distributed to the Scouts. Agree upon recall signals so the search does not continue after the lost child has been found.

The search will be more dramatic and realistic if you or your Scoutmaster can make arrangements with a military unit or police department to use walkie-talkies in coordinating the search.

Have Scouts look for the prepared evidence of the lost child. Once found, the lost child should be properly treated for any injuries and transported safely to the starting point.

Messenger Service Project

Operating a messenger service is one way Scouts can give meaningful service during an emergency and help to free community officials so that they can concentrate on their specialized skills. This project will test the ability of your troop to organize and work as a team.

At a convenient time (a weekday evening, perhaps, or a Saturday afternoon), call an emergency mobilization of the troop. When all patrols are at the unit meeting place, give each patrol leader a list of 10 to 15 prominent places in the community, such as police and fire stations, drugstores, service stations, and places of business or government. (Use a different list of contacts for each patrol so that busy people are not disturbed repeatedly to sign messages.) Give each patrol leader enough copies of this suggested note to cover the list.

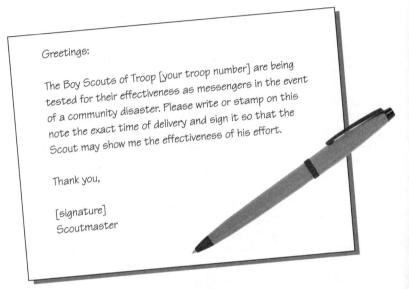

Greetings:

The Boy Scouts of Troop [your troop number] are being tested for their effectiveness as messengers in the event of a community disaster. Please write or stamp on this note the exact time of delivery and sign it so that the Scout may show me the effectiveness of his effort.

Thank you,

[signature]
Scoutmaster

If you hold this mobilization in the evening, you could end it with a special campfire program.

Other Projects

With the help of your Scoutmaster and other troop leaders, you can follow the same approach as for the preceding projects to alert your troop leaders to select, plan for, and participate in an emergency service project. Other action projects that will help you and your troop sharpen emergency skills might include conducting a simulated, or mock, bicycle or car accident, or setting up an emergency camp from scratch (with sanitation, cooking, and dishwashing facilities for a large number of people). Or you might simulate a building accident or fire, with "victims" role-playing such emergencies as touching a live electrical wire, having their clothes on fire, or experiencing stopped breathing.

Emergency Preparedness Resources

Your local library is always a good starting place as you search for information and resources. A good troop project would be to go to your library and make a list of at least 10 emergency preparedness resources that you can use as you complete the requirements for the Emergency Preparedness merit badge.

Scouting Literature

Backpacking, Camping, Canoeing, Cooking, Cycling, Electricity, Fire Safety, First Aid, Hiking, Home Repairs, Lifesaving, Motorboating, Nature, Orienteering, Pioneering, Public Health, Radio, Rowing, Safety, Small-Boat Sailing, Snow Sports, Swimming, Traffic Safety, Weather, and *Wilderness Survival* merit badge pamphlets

Books

Forgey, William W. *The Basic Essentials of First Aid for the Outdoors* (Basic Essentials Series). ICS Books, 1989.

Handel, M.D., Kathleen. *The American Red Cross First Aid and Safety Handbook.* Little Brown & Company, 1992.

Kelly, Kate. *Living Safe in an Unsafe World: The Complete Guide to Family Preparedness.* New American Library Trade, 2000.

Mason, Rosalie. *Beginners Guide to Family Preparedness.* Horizon Publishers & Distributors, 1977.

Meyer-Crissey, Pamela, and Brian L. Crissey, Ph.D. *Common Sense in Uncommon Times.* Granite Publishing, 2002.

Roskind, Robert A. *The Complete Emergency Home Preparation Guide.* Prentice Hall Professional Technical Reference, 1999.

Salsbury, Barbara G. *Just in Case: A Manual of Home Preparedness.* Bookcraft, 1980.

Organizations, Government Agencies, and Web Sites

American Red Cross
Toll-free telephone: 877-272-7337
Web site: *http://www.redcross.org*

The American Red Cross is a humanitarian organization associated with the International Red Cross Movement that provides relief to victims of disasters and helps people prevent, prepare for, and respond to emergencies. Know where the closest local Red Cross chapter is in your area and what services and information they can provide. On its Web site, the Red Cross has information about disaster services (*http://www.redcross.org/services/disaster*) that covers topics such as how to be prepared for disaster, how families can plan for disaster, and safety considerations after a disaster. To locate the chapter nearest you, visit the ARC Web site or call the toll-free number.

Environmental Hazards Management Institute
Toll-free telephone: 800-446-5256
Web site: *http://www.ehmi.org*

The Environmental Hazards Management Institute, founded in 1979, is a nonpartisan, nonprofit environmental, health, safety, and sustainability education and research organization working to promote environmental responsibility at home, in the workplace, and in the community through education and relationship building. Contact the EHMI to obtain educational materials.

Environmental Protection Agency

Ariel Rios Building
1200 Pennsylvania Avenue NW
Washington, DC 20460
Telephone: 202-260-2090
Toll-free telephone for literature requests only: 800-490-9198
Web site: *http://www.epa.gov*

The Environmental Protection Agency works to prevent, prepare for, and respond to spills and other environmental emergencies. Its Web site provides information about these activities, links to the key groups involved in contingency planning and response, and information on how to report hazardous substance and oil spills. Its Web site has a section about environmental emergencies (*http://www. epa.gov/ebtpages/emergencies.html*), which would include the release or threatened release of oil, radioactive materials, or hazardous chemicals that may affect communities and the environment. Visit the EPA Web site or call to locate the regional office nearest you. You can order EPA publications online or by calling the toll-free number.

Federal Emergency Management Agency

500 C Street, SW
Washington, DC 20472
Telephone: 202-566-1600
Toll-free telephone for literature requests only: 800-480-2520
Web site: *http://www.fema.gov*

The Federal Emergency Management Agency is an independent agency that reports to the president and has the task of responding to, planning for, recovering from, and lessening disaster. It traces its beginnings to the first piece of disaster legislation in our government—a Congressional Act in 1803 that provided help to a town in New Hampshire after a fire. Lots of disaster information is available online, along with an "electronic reading room" (*http://www.fema.gov/library*) that includes information on preparedness, response, and recovery.

National Oceanic and Atmospheric Administration
14th Street and Constitution Avenue, NW
Washington, DC 20230
Telephone: 202-482-6090
Web site: *http://www.noaa.gov*

The National Oceanic and Atmospheric Administration was established in 1970 "for better protection of life and property from natural hazards . . . for a better understanding of the total environment . . . [and] for exploration and development leading to the intelligent use of our marine resources." You can learn a lot about climate and the weather by visiting its Web site.

National Weather Service
U.S. Department of Commerce
National Oceanic and Atmospheric Administration
1325 East West Highway
Silver Spring, MD 20910
Web site: *http://www.nws.noaa.gov*

The National Weather Service is part of NOAA and has many brochures and publications available online (*http://www.nws.noaa.gov/om/brochures.shtml*), or you can order a free copy of most publications from a local NWS office, NOAA Outreach Unit, or local American Red Cross chapter. You will find information on emergency preparedness, boating, and all weather-related disasters.

U.S. Geological Survey
Toll-free telephone: 888-ASK-USGS (or 888-275-8747)
Web site: *http://www.usgs.gov*

The U.S. Geological Survey has the mission of providing reliable scientific information to help describe and understand the Earth; minimize loss of life and property from natural disasters; manage water, biological, energy, and mineral resources; and enhance and protect our quality of life. It has offices throughout the country. For information, call the toll-free number or visit the USGS Web site.

Acknowledgements

The Boy Scouts of America is grateful to the American Red Cross for its assistance with updating this new edition of the *Emergency Preparedness* merit badge pamphlet. In particular, we are grateful to Rocky Lopes, Ph.D., who serves as the ARC's senior associate of community disaster education. Dr. Lopes provided his time and expertise and was instrumental to this revised edition. Thanks also to the Dallas (Texas) Area Chapter of the American Red Cross for its assistance with photography for the cover of this new edition.

Thanks to the American Library Association for its assistance with updating the resources section of this pamphlet. For many years, the ALA has had a special committee that helps the BSA with its merit badge pamphlet series in this capacity, and it does so very effectively.

Photo and Art Credits

BSA Risk Management, courtesy—page 15

Joseph Csatari—page 9

Digital Stock, ©1996—page 39

Daniel Giles—page 17

Ingram Publishing, ©1994–2001—pages 26, 40, 53 (all), 79, and 82

Roy Jansen—page 65

Frank McMahon—page 73

Brian Payne—pages 25 (top), 28, and 56

Randy Piland—page 33

Steve Seeger—page 48

Scott Stenjem—page 29

Three Mile Island, courtesy—page 54

Notes